PAULINE PRINCIPLES OF RESTORATIVE JUSTICE

Dr. Maxwell Shimba

Printed in the United States of America

TABLE OF CONTENTS

INTRODUCTION

Restorative justice is a transformative concept that emphasizes restoring relationships, repairing harm, and reintegrating offenders into the community. This approach contrasts sharply with retributive justice, which centers on punishment and retribution. In the restorative justice paradigm, the focus shifts from punishment to healing, reconciliation, and the restoration of community harmony.

The teachings of Apostle Paul in the New Testament offer a profound foundation for understanding and applying restorative justice within Christian communities. Paul's epistles are rich with themes and principles that resonate with restorative justice, providing guidance on how to mend broken relationships, seek forgiveness, and promote reconciliation.

Apostle Paul's life, from his dramatic conversion on the road to Damascus to his tireless work as a missionary and theologian, exemplifies the principles of restorative justice. His writings to the early Christian communities addressed conflicts, called for forgiveness, and emphasized the importance of love and reconciliation. These teachings remain relevant today, offering a timeless framework for addressing harm and fostering healing in our communities.

This book delves into the restorative justice principles found in Paul's epistles, examining how his teachings can be applied to modern Christian life. Through careful analysis of Paul's letters, we will explore how concepts of forgiveness, reconciliation, accountability, and community support are interwoven into his theological framework.

We will begin by understanding the broader context of restorative justice, its principles, and how it compares to retributive justice. We will then explore the theological foundations of restorative justice, drawing from both the Old and New Testaments. Following this, we will examine Paul's personal transformation and how it mirrors restorative justice principles.

Subsequent chapters will delve into Paul's teachings on forgiveness, reconciliation, community accountability, and the balance of justice and mercy. We will also explore Paul's personal appeal for restorative justice in his letter to Philemon, showcasing a practical example of how these principles were applied in a real-life situation.

The role of love, a central theme in Paul's theology, will be highlighted as a foundational element for restorative justice. We will address common barriers to implementing restorative justice and offer strategies for overcoming these challenges. Finally, we will look at contemporary applications of Paul's teachings, providing practical insights for modern church settings and ministries.

Through this exploration, we aim to provide a comprehensive understanding of restorative justice through the lens of Apostle Paul's teachings. This book is not just an academic exercise but a practical guide for individuals and communities seeking to embody these transformative principles in their lives. By embracing restorative justice, we can foster a culture of healing, reconciliation, and genuine community restoration, reflecting the heart of Paul's message and the teachings of Christ.

Dr. Maxwell Shimba

DR. MAXWELL SHIMBA

CHAPTER 01

UNDERSTANDING RESTORATIVE JUSTICE

Definition and Principles of Restorative Justice

Restorative justice is a concept that transcends mere punishment and seeks to address the root causes of harm, repair damaged relationships, and reintegrate offenders into the community. This chapter aims to provide a comprehensive understanding of restorative justice, its definitions, and its core principles.

Restorative justice is often defined as a process that brings together those who have been harmed, those responsible for the harm, and the wider community to collectively address and resolve the aftermath of an offense. Unlike retributive justice, which focuses on the punishment of the offender, restorative justice emphasizes healing, accountability, and the restoration of relationships.

According to Howard Zehr, a pioneer in the field, restorative justice can be summarized with three key questions:

1. Who has been harmed?

2. What are their needs?

3. Whose obligations are these?

This approach shifts the focus from what laws were broken and what punishment is deserved, to who has been affected by the harm and how that harm can be addressed.

Principles of Restorative Justice

Restorative justice is grounded in several key principles that guide its practices and goals:

1. Repairing Harm

At the heart of restorative justice is the commitment to repair the harm caused by criminal behavior. This involves addressing the needs of the victims, the offenders, and the community. Victims' needs might include receiving an apology, understanding why the harm occurred, and having a say in how the harm is repaired. Offenders are encouraged to take responsibility for their actions and make amends, which can lead to their own rehabilitation and reintegration into society.

2. Involvement of Stakeholders

Restorative justice involves all stakeholders affected by the offense – victims, offenders, and the community. This inclusive approach ensures that all voices are heard and considered in the process of addressing the harm. The involvement of the community underscores the idea that crime affects more than just the direct victim; it impacts the social fabric of the community.

3. Transformation of Relationships

Restorative justice aims to transform relationships that have been damaged by crime. This transformation is achieved through processes that promote understanding, dialogue, and mutual agreement on how to move forward. By addressing the underlying issues that led to the harm, restorative justice seeks to prevent future offenses and build stronger, healthier communities.

4. Voluntary Participation

Participation in restorative justice processes must be voluntary for all parties involved. Coercing victims or offenders into the process can undermine its effectiveness and the genuine healing it seeks to promote. Voluntary participation ensures that the process is based on mutual consent and respect.

5. Accountability and Responsibility

Restorative justice emphasizes the importance of accountability and responsibility. Offenders are encouraged to acknowledge the harm they have caused and take steps to make things right. This accountability is not about punishment but about understanding the impact of their actions and working towards restoration.

6. Reintegration

A key goal of restorative justice is the reintegration of offenders into the community. Rather than being ostracized or permanently labeled, offenders are given the opportunity to make amends and rebuild their lives. This reintegration is crucial for breaking the cycle of crime and fostering long-term positive change.

Restorative Justice in Practice

Restorative justice can be implemented through various practices and processes. Some of the most common methods include:

1. Victim-Offender Mediation

Victim-offender mediation involves a facilitated dialogue between the victim and the offender. This process allows the victim to express how the crime affected them and gives the offender a chance to take responsibility and offer an apology. Together, they work towards a mutually agreed-upon resolution.

2. Restorative Circles

Restorative circles bring together the victim, offender, community members, and sometimes even family members in a circle dialogue. This process fosters open communication, mutual understanding, and collective decision-making. It aims to heal relationships and address the broader impact of the harm.

3. Family Group Conferencing

Family group conferencing involves a meeting between the victim, offender, their families, and sometimes other community members. The focus is on supporting the victim and holding the offender accountable while involving their support network in the process of making amends and planning for the future.

4. Community Reparative Boards

Community reparative boards consist of community members who meet with the offender to discuss the impact of the crime and agree on actions the offender can take to make amends. This process emphasizes community involvement and support for the offender's reintegration.

The Benefits of Restorative Justice

Restorative justice offers numerous benefits for victims, offenders, and communities:

1. For Victims

- Provides a sense of closure and healing.

- Allows victims to express their feelings and be heard.

- Offers an opportunity for victims to have a say in how the harm is repaired.

2. For Offenders

- Encourages personal accountability and responsibility.

- Provides an opportunity to make amends and rebuild their lives.

- Reduces recidivism by addressing the root causes of criminal behavior.

3. For Communities

- Strengthens community ties and fosters a sense of collective responsibility.

- Reduces the social and economic costs of crime.

- Promotes a more compassionate and just society.

Restorative justice is a powerful approach that goes beyond punishment to address the needs of victims, offenders, and communities. Its principles of repairing harm, involving stakeholders, transforming relationships, voluntary participation, accountability, and reintegration offer a holistic framework for addressing crime and fostering healing.

As we explore the teachings of Apostle Paul in subsequent chapters, we will see how his epistles resonate with these principles and provide timeless guidance for implementing restorative justice in our lives and communities. Through Paul's teachings, we can gain a deeper understanding of how to build a more just, compassionate, and restorative society.

HISTORICAL CONTEXT AND DEVELOPMENT OF RESTORATIVE JUSTICE

Understanding the historical context and development of restorative justice provides essential insights into its foundational principles and how it has evolved over time. This chapter explores the origins of restorative justice, its practices in ancient and traditional societies, and its resurgence in modern times.

Ancient and Traditional Roots

Restorative Practices in Ancient Societies

Restorative justice is not a new concept; its roots can be traced back to ancient civilizations where communities sought to resolve conflicts and restore harmony through collective processes.

1. Ancient Israel: The Old Testament provides numerous examples of restorative practices. For instance, the law of restitution in Exodus 22:1-14 outlines how offenders should compensate victims for their losses. This approach

focused on making the victim whole rather than punishing the offender. The concept of "Shalom," meaning peace and wholeness, underscores the importance of restoring relationships and community harmony.

2. Greece and Rome: In ancient Greece and Rome, community-based approaches to justice were common. The Greeks practiced a form of mediation where respected community members facilitated discussions between conflicting parties. The Romans employed a system of compensation for certain offenses, emphasizing the restoration of the victim's status and property.

3. Indigenous Cultures: Indigenous cultures around the world have long practiced forms of restorative justice. For example, the Maori of New Zealand use a process called "Whanau Conferencing," where family members gather to discuss the harm and collectively decide on a resolution. Similarly, many Native American tribes have traditions of healing circles and peacemaking, where the focus is on restoring harmony and balance within the community.

The Role of Religion and Philosophy

Religious and philosophical traditions have also played a significant role in shaping restorative justice principles.

1. Judaism and Christianity: In addition to the examples from the Old Testament, the New Testament

emphasizes forgiveness, reconciliation, and restorative practices. Jesus' teachings on forgiveness (Matthew 18:21-22) and reconciliation (Matthew 5:23-24) highlight the importance of mending relationships and seeking peace.

2. Buddhism and Hinduism: In Eastern philosophies, the concepts of karma and dharma stress the interconnectedness of actions and their consequences. Restorative practices in these traditions often involve acknowledging harm, seeking forgiveness, and making amends to restore balance.

3. Islam: The Quran and Hadiths also emphasize justice, forgiveness, and reconciliation. The concept of "Sulh" (reconciliation) is a critical aspect of Islamic justice, encouraging mediation and amicable settlements to resolve conflicts and repair relationships.

Medieval and Early Modern Periods

During the medieval and early modern periods, restorative practices continued to coexist with retributive justice systems.

Medieval Europe

1. Feudal System: In medieval Europe, the feudal system involved lords and vassals resolving disputes within their domains. While punishment was common, restorative

practices such as compensation and reconciliation were also used to maintain social order and stability.

2. Canon Law: The Catholic Church's canon law incorporated restorative elements, emphasizing penance, confession, and reconciliation. These practices aimed to restore the sinner's relationship with God and the community.

Indigenous and Colonial Contexts

1. Indigenous Justice Systems: Indigenous communities in the Americas, Africa, and other regions maintained their restorative practices even under colonial rule. These systems often clashed with the retributive justice systems imposed by colonizers.

2. Colonial Impact: Colonial powers introduced Western legal systems that prioritized punishment over restoration. However, indigenous practices persisted and continued to influence local justice systems.

The Resurgence of Restorative Justice in Modern Times

The modern restorative justice movement began to take shape in the 20th century, driven by a growing dissatisfaction with the limitations of retributive justice and the desire for more humane and effective approaches.

Influential Theories and Movements

1. Howard Zehr: Often referred to as the "grandfather of restorative justice," Howard Zehr's work has been instrumental in defining and promoting restorative justice. His book, "Changing Lenses," published in 1990, provided a new framework for understanding justice, focusing on healing and restoration rather than punishment.

2. Victim-Offender Reconciliation Programs (VORP): One of the earliest modern restorative justice programs was the Victim-Offender Reconciliation Program, which began in Canada in the 1970s. These programs brought victims and offenders together to discuss the harm and work towards a resolution, laying the groundwork for contemporary restorative practices.

3. Peacemaking Criminology: This movement, emerging in the late 20th century, emphasized nonviolent responses to crime and conflict. It drew from various traditions, including indigenous practices, religious teachings, and alternative dispute-resolution methods.

Global Adoption and Institutionalization

Restorative justice has gained traction worldwide, with various countries and communities adopting and institutionalizing restorative practices.

1. New Zealand: New Zealand is a leading example of restorative justice implementation. The country has integrated

restorative practices into its juvenile justice system, emphasizing family group conferencing and community involvement.

2. South Africa: In the aftermath of apartheid, South Africa's Truth and Reconciliation Commission (TRC) became a landmark restorative justice initiative. The TRC focused on uncovering the truth, acknowledging harm, and promoting national healing and reconciliation.

3. United States and Canada: Restorative justice programs have been established in schools, prisons, and communities across the United States and Canada. These programs aim to address harm, reduce recidivism, and build stronger communities.

4. Europe: Various European countries, including Norway, the United Kingdom, and the Netherlands, have adopted restorative justice practices within their criminal justice systems. These initiatives range from victim-offender mediation to restorative circles and community reparative boards.

The historical context and development of restorative justice reveal its deep roots in ancient and traditional societies, its persistence through medieval and early modern periods, and its resurgence in modern times. Understanding this history provides a rich foundation for appreciating the principles and practices of restorative justice and their relevance in addressing contemporary challenges.

As we move forward in this book, we will explore how the teachings of Apostle Paul align with these principles and how they can be applied to promote healing, reconciliation, and restoration in our communities. Through this exploration, we aim to uncover timeless wisdom that can guide us in building a more just and compassionate society.

COMPARISON WITH RETRIBUTIVE JUSTICE

To fully appreciate the principles of restorative justice, it is essential to understand how it compares to retributive justice, the dominant paradigm in many contemporary legal systems. Retributive justice focuses on punishment as a response to crime, while restorative justice emphasizes healing, reconciliation, and the restoration of relationships. This chapter will explore the key differences between these two approaches, their underlying philosophies, and the implications of each for individuals and communities.

The Philosophical Foundations of Retributive Justice

Definition and Key Concepts

Retributive justice is based on the principle that offenders should be punished for their crimes in proportion to the severity of their offenses. This approach is rooted in the belief that punishment serves as a deterrent, satisfies a societal need for retribution, and upholds the moral order by ensuring that wrongdoers receive their just deserts.

Key concepts of retributive justice include:

1. Desert: Offenders deserve to be punished because they have committed a moral wrong. The punishment is seen as a justified response to the offense.

2. Proportionality: The severity of the punishment should be proportionate to the seriousness of the crime. This principle aims to ensure fairness and consistency in sentencing.

3. Deterrence: Punishment serves to deter both the individual offender and others in society from committing similar offenses in the future.

4. Retribution: Punishment is viewed as a necessary response to wrongdoing, reflecting society's condemnation of the offense and reaffirming moral values.

Historical Development

Retributive justice has deep historical roots, dating back to ancient legal codes such as the Code of Hammurabi, which emphasized the principle of "an eye for an eye." This concept was further developed in Roman law and later in the legal traditions of Western societies.

Throughout history, retributive justice has been reinforced by philosophical and theological perspectives. For example, Immanuel Kant argued that punishment is a moral imperative, necessary to uphold justice and respect for the law. Similarly, the retributive principles found in the Old Testament reflect a view that punishment is essential to maintain social order and justice.

The Philosophical Foundations of Restorative Justice

Definition and Key Concepts

Restorative justice, in contrast, focuses on repairing the harm caused by criminal behavior and restoring relationships. This approach seeks to address the needs of victims, hold offenders accountable in a constructive manner, and involve the community in the process of healing and reconciliation.

Key concepts of restorative justice include:

1. Repairing Harm: The primary goal is to address the harm caused by the offense and find ways to make amends. This often involves restitution, apologies, and other actions that contribute to healing.

2. Accountability: Offenders are encouraged to take responsibility for their actions and understand the impact of their behavior on victims and the community.

3. Involvement of Stakeholders: Restorative justice involves all affected parties, including victims, offenders, and community members, in the process of finding solutions and addressing the harm.

4. Reintegration: The approach aims to reintegrate offenders into the community, helping them to rebuild their lives and relationships in a positive manner.

Historical Development

Restorative justice has roots in various ancient and traditional practices, as discussed in previous sections. It has been influenced by indigenous justice systems, religious teachings, and philosophical perspectives that emphasize reconciliation and community harmony.

In modern times, the restorative justice movement gained momentum in the latter half of the 20th century, driven by a growing recognition of the limitations of retributive justice and a desire for more humane and effective approaches to addressing crime.

Key Differences Between Retributive and Restorative Justice

Goals and Outcomes

1. Retributive Justice: The primary goal is to punish the offender and uphold the rule of law. The focus is on establishing guilt and imposing a penalty that reflects the

severity of the crime. The outcome is often incarceration, fines, or other forms of punishment.

2. Restorative Justice: The primary goal is to repair the harm and restore relationships. The focus is on healing for the victim, accountability for the offender, and community involvement in the resolution process. The outcome often includes restitution, community service, and other actions that contribute to reconciliation and reintegration.

Approach to Offenders

1. Retributive Justice: Offenders are viewed as individuals who have broken the law and must be punished. The process is adversarial, with the state prosecuting the offender and the offender defending against the charges.

2. Restorative Justice: Offenders are viewed as individuals who have caused harm and need to take responsibility for their actions. The process is collaborative, involving dialogue and negotiation between the victim, offender, and community members.

Role of Victims

1. Retributive Justice: Victims often have a limited role, primarily as witnesses in the prosecution of the offender. The focus is on the crime and the punishment, with less attention to the needs and perspectives of the victim.

2. Restorative Justice: Victims play a central role in the process. Their needs, perspectives, and experiences are integral to finding a resolution. They have the opportunity to express their feelings, ask questions, and participate in deciding how the harm should be addressed.

Community Involvement

1. Retributive Justice: The community is largely excluded from the process, with the state acting as the primary agent of justice. The focus is on the legal aspects of the crime rather than the broader social impact.

2. Restorative Justice: The community is actively involved in the process, contributing to the resolution and supporting both the victim and the offender. The focus is on restoring community harmony and addressing the social dimensions of the harm.

Criticisms and Challenges

Criticisms of Retributive Justice

1. Ineffectiveness: Critics argue that retributive justice often fails to prevent reoffending and does not address the underlying causes of crime.

2. Harm to Offenders: Punitive measures can have long-lasting negative effects on offenders, including stigmatization, social exclusion, and difficulties in reintegration.

3. Neglect of Victims: The retributive system is often criticized for neglecting the needs and voices of victims, focusing more on punishment than on healing.

Criticisms of Restorative Justice

1. Perceived Leniency: Some argue that restorative justice can be too lenient on offenders, potentially undermining the deterrent effect of punishment.

2. Implementation Challenges: Effective implementation of restorative justice requires skilled facilitators, supportive communities, and willing participants, which can be difficult to achieve.

3. Consistency and Fairness: Ensuring consistency and fairness in restorative justice practices can be challenging, as outcomes are often tailored to the specific circumstances of each case.

Retributive justice and restorative justice represent two fundamentally different approaches to addressing crime and harm. While retributive justice focuses on punishment and upholding the law, restorative justice emphasizes healing, reconciliation, and the restoration of relationships.

Understanding these differences is crucial for appreciating the potential of restorative justice to transform our approach to crime and conflict. As we continue to explore the teachings of Apostle Paul, we will see how his epistles align with the principles of restorative justice and offer timeless guidance for building more just and compassionate communities. Through this exploration, we aim to uncover practical insights and applications that can help us move beyond punishment towards a more restorative and humane vision of justice.

THE ROLE OF COMMUNITY AND RECONCILIATION

The role of community and reconciliation is central to the concept of restorative justice. Unlike retributive justice, which often isolates the offender from the community, restorative justice seeks to involve the community in the process of addressing harm, promoting healing, and restoring relationships. This chapter explores the importance of community involvement in restorative justice and the process of reconciliation that aims to mend the fabric of society torn by crime.

The Importance of Community in Restorative Justice

Community as a Stakeholder

In restorative justice, the community is seen as a key stakeholder in the justice process. Crime is not viewed merely as a violation of law but as a breach of the relationships and social harmony within the community. Therefore, the community has a vested interest in the resolution of crime and the restoration of peace.

1. Collective Responsibility: Restorative justice recognizes that communities have a collective responsibility to address crime and its impacts. This collective approach helps to distribute the burden of addressing harm and ensures that the community plays a supportive role in the healing process.

2. Social Capital: Community involvement builds social capital, fostering trust and cooperation among members. When a community collectively works towards justice, it strengthens its social bonds and resilience against future harms.

Community Participation in Restorative Processes

Community participation can take various forms in restorative justice processes, including:

1. Restorative Circles: Community members participate in restorative circles, where they discuss the impact of the crime, support the victim and offender, and collectively decide on steps to repair the harm. This inclusive process ensures that all voices are heard and respected.

2. Community Reparative Boards: These boards consist of community volunteers who meet with the offender to discuss the offense and agree on actions to make amends.

The involvement of community members in these boards emphasizes the community's role in holding the offender accountable and supporting their reintegration.

3. Family Group Conferencing: This process brings together the victim, offender, their families, and sometimes community members to discuss the harm and find a resolution. The inclusion of family and community in the discussion underscores the interconnectedness of relationships and the community's role in supporting both the victim and the offender.

The Process of Reconciliation

Definition and Goals of Reconciliation

Reconciliation is the process of restoring relationships and achieving harmony after a conflict or harm. In the context of restorative justice, reconciliation involves:

1. Acknowledgment of Harm: Recognizing the harm caused by the offense and its impact on the victim, offender, and community.

2. Restoration of Relationships: Working towards mending the damaged relationships and rebuilding trust among the affected parties.

3. Promotion of Healing: Facilitating emotional and psychological healing for the victim, offender, and community members.

Steps to Reconciliation

Reconciliation in restorative justice typically involves several steps:

1. Preparation and Dialogue: Before the reconciliation process begins, preparatory meetings are often held to ensure that all parties are ready to engage in a constructive dialogue. This preparation helps to set the stage for a respectful and open conversation.

2. Facilitated Meetings: A trained facilitator guides the reconciliation meetings, ensuring that everyone has an opportunity to speak and that the conversation remains focused on healing and resolution. The facilitator's role is to create a safe space for honest and empathetic communication.

3. Expression of Impact: During the meetings, the victim has the opportunity to express how the offense has affected them. This expression is crucial for acknowledging the harm and validating the victim's experience.

4. Acceptance of Responsibility: The offender is encouraged to accept responsibility for their actions and acknowledge the harm they have caused. This acceptance is a critical step towards genuine accountability and remorse.

5. Restorative Agreements: The parties collaboratively develop a plan to address the harm and make amends. This

plan may include actions such as restitution, community service, or other forms of reparative work.

6. Follow-Up and Support: After the initial reconciliation meeting, follow-up meetings and ongoing support are essential to ensure that the restorative agreements are implemented and that the healing process continues. This follow-up helps to reinforce the commitment to reconciliation and monitor progress.

The Role of Community in Supporting Reconciliation

Providing Emotional and Practical Support

The community plays a vital role in supporting both the victim and the offender during and after the reconciliation process. This support can take various forms:

1. Emotional Support: Community members can offer emotional support by listening, empathizing, and providing encouragement to both the victim and the offender. This support helps to foster a sense of belonging and reduces feelings of isolation.

2. Practical Assistance: Communities can provide practical assistance, such as helping the offender find employment or housing, offering counseling services, or assisting the victim with any ongoing needs related to the offense. This practical support is crucial for the successful

reintegration of the offender and the continued healing of the victim.

Building a Culture of Reconciliation

Creating a culture of reconciliation within the community involves promoting values and practices that support restorative justice principles. This can be achieved through:

1. Education and Awareness: Educating community members about restorative justice and its benefits helps to build understanding and support for restorative practices. This education can be provided through workshops, seminars, and community events.

2. Community Engagement: Actively engaging community members in restorative justice processes and decision-making fosters a sense of ownership and responsibility. This engagement helps to ensure that restorative practices are tailored to the specific needs and values of the community.

3. Promoting Restorative Values: Encouraging values such as empathy, forgiveness, and mutual respect within the community helps to create an environment conducive to reconciliation. These values can be promoted through community initiatives, faith-based organizations, and local leadership.

Case Studies of Community and Reconciliation in Action

New Zealand's Family Group Conferencing

New Zealand's Family Group Conferencing (FGC) is a pioneering example of community involvement in restorative justice. The FGC model involves the victim, offender, their families, and community representatives in a facilitated meeting to discuss the harm and develop a plan for restitution. This process emphasizes the importance of family and community support in achieving reconciliation and successful reintegration of the offender.

South Africa's Truth and Reconciliation Commission

South Africa's Truth and Reconciliation Commission (TRC) is a landmark example of reconciliation on a national scale. Established after the end of apartheid, the TRC provided a platform for victims and perpetrators to share their experiences, acknowledge the harm, and work towards healing. The involvement of the broader South African community in the TRC process highlighted the critical role of collective engagement in achieving reconciliation and rebuilding a fractured society.

The role of community and reconciliation is central to the philosophy and practice of restorative justice. By involving the community in the justice process and focusing on reconciliation, restorative justice seeks to repair harm, restore relationships, and promote healing for all parties affected by crime. Understanding and embracing these principles can help communities build stronger, more resilient social bonds and create a more just and compassionate society.

As we continue to explore the teachings of Apostle Paul, we will see how his epistles align with these principles and offer timeless guidance for fostering community involvement and reconciliation. Through this exploration, we aim to uncover practical insights and applications that can help us move beyond punishment toward a more restorative and humane vision of justice.

CHAPTER 02

THE THEOLOGY FOUNDATION OF RESTORATIVE JUSTICE

Biblical Basis for Restorative Justice

The concept of restorative justice is deeply rooted in biblical teachings. Both the Old and New Testaments provide numerous examples and principles that align with restorative justice. This chapter explores the biblical foundations of restorative justice, demonstrating how scripture supports the principles of healing, reconciliation, and restoration.

Restorative Justice in the Old Testament

The Law of Moses

The Law of Moses, as outlined in the Pentateuch, contains many provisions that emphasize restitution and restoration rather than mere punishment.

1. Restitution for Theft: In Exodus 22:1-4, the law prescribes that a thief must make restitution by repaying multiple times the value of what was stolen. This principle focuses on making the victim whole rather than simply punishing the offender.

If a man steals an ox or a sheep and kills it or sells it, he shall repay five oxen for an ox and four sheep for a sheep. (Exodus 22:1)

2. Restitution for Property Damage: Leviticus 6:1-5 requires that anyone who damages or takes another person's property must make full restitution and add a fifth of the value as compensation. This law emphasizes repairing the harm caused and restoring the relationship between the parties.

He shall restore it in full and shall add a fifth to it. (Leviticus 6:5)

3. Cities of Refuge: Numbers 35:9-34 describes the establishment of cities of refuge where individuals who committed unintentional manslaughter could seek asylum. This provision protected the offender from revenge while ensuring that justice was served through a fair trial. The Cities of Refuge highlights the importance of mercy, protection, and due process in the administration of justice.

Then you shall select cities to be cities of refuge for you, that the manslayer who kills any person without intent may flee there. (Numbers 35:11)

Prophetic Calls for Justice and Mercy

The prophets of the Old Testament frequently called for justice, mercy, and reconciliation, reflecting the principles of restorative justice.

1. Isaiah's Vision of Justice: Isaiah 1:17 urges the people to seek justice, correct oppression, and defend the cause of the vulnerable. This vision emphasizes active involvement in creating a just and compassionate society.

Learn to do good; seek justice, correct oppression; bring justice to the fatherless, plead the widow's cause. (Isaiah 1:17)

2. Micah's Call for Justice and Mercy: Micah 6:8 encapsulates the essence of restorative justice by calling for individuals to act justly, love mercy, and walk humbly with God.

He has told you, O man, what is good; and what does the Lord require of you but to do justice, and to love kindness, and to walk humbly with your God? (Micah 6:8)

Restorative Justice in the New Testament

Jesus' Teachings on Forgiveness and Reconciliation

The teachings of Jesus in the New Testament provide a profound foundation for restorative justice, emphasizing forgiveness, reconciliation, and love.

1. The Parable of the Prodigal Son: In Luke 15:11-32, Jesus tells the parable of the prodigal son, illustrating the themes of repentance, forgiveness, and reconciliation. The father's unconditional love and willingness to restore his wayward son to the family underscore the principles of restorative justice.

But while he was still a long way off, his father saw him and felt compassion, and ran and embraced him and kissed him. (Luke 15:20)

2. Teaching on Forgiveness: In Matthew 18:21-22, Jesus emphasizes the importance of limitless forgiveness, teaching that one should forgive not just seven times but seventy-seven times. This teaching highlights the centrality of forgiveness in restoring relationships.

Jesus said to him, "I do not say to you seven times, but seventy-seven times. (Matthew 18:22)

3. Reconciliation with Others: In Matthew 5:23-24, Jesus instructs his followers to seek reconciliation with others before offering gifts at the altar, demonstrating the priority of mending relationships.

So if you are offering your gift at the altar and there remember that your brother has something against you, leave your gift there before the altar and go. First be reconciled to your brother, and then come and offer your gift. (Matthew 5:23-24)

The Apostolic Teachings on Justice and Reconciliation

The teachings of the apostles, particularly Paul, further elucidate the principles of restorative justice.

1. Paul's Call for Reconciliation: In 2 Corinthians 5:18-20, Paul speaks of the ministry of reconciliation, highlighting that believers are called to be agents of reconciliation in the world. This ministry reflects the heart of restorative justice, focusing on restoring relationships with God and others.

All this is from God, who through Christ reconciled us to himself and gave us the ministry of reconciliation. (2 Corinthians 5:18)

2. Restoring a Sinning Believer: In Galatians 6:1-2, Paul advises believers to restore those caught in sin with a spirit of gentleness, emphasizing restoration and support rather than punishment.

Brothers, if anyone is caught in any transgression, you who are spiritual should restore him in a spirit of gentleness.

Keep watch on yourself, lest you too be tempted. (Galatians 6:1)

3. Forgiveness and Comfort: In 2 Corinthians 2:5-8, Paul urges the church to forgive and comfort a repentant sinner to prevent overwhelming sorrow, demonstrating the importance of compassion and support in the process of restoration.

So you should rather turn to forgive and comfort him, or he may be overwhelmed by excessive sorrow. So I beg you to reaffirm your love for him. (2 Corinthians 2:7-8)

The Early Church and Restorative Practices

Community Support and Accountability

The early Christian communities modeled restorative principles through their practices of mutual support, accountability, and communal living.

1. Sharing of Resources: Acts 2:44-45 describes the early believers sharing their possessions and resources, ensuring that no one in the community was in need. This practice reflects the principles of mutual care and support, which are essential to restorative justice.

And all who believed were together and had all things in common. And they were selling their possessions and belongings and distributing the proceeds to all, as any had need. (Acts 2:44-45)

2. Addressing Conflicts: In Matthew 18:15-17, Jesus provides a process for addressing conflicts within the community, emphasizing reconciliation and restoration over punishment. This process involves private correction, involving witnesses, and finally bringing the matter before the church if necessary.

If your brother sins against you, go and tell him his fault, between you and him alone. If he listens to you, you have gained your brother. (Matthew 18:15)

3. Church Discipline: The early church practiced restorative discipline, aiming to correct and restore rather than merely punish. In 1 Corinthians 5:1-5, Paul addresses a case of serious immorality in the church, recommending a process that ultimately aims at the offender's repentance and restoration.

You are to deliver this man to Satan for the destruction of the flesh, so that his spirit may be saved in the day of the Lord. (1 Corinthians 5:5)

Theological Themes Underpinning Restorative Justice

The Image of God

The belief that all humans are created in the image of God (Imago Dei) underpins the respect and dignity afforded to every individual, including offenders. This theological concept supports restorative justice by emphasizing the inherent worth of every person and the need for restoration rather than mere retribution.

1. Human Dignity: Genesis 1:27 highlights that every person is made in the image of God, affirming their value and dignity. This belief encourages a restorative approach that seeks to honor and restore rather than demean and punish.

So, God created man in his image, in the image of God he created him; male and female he created them. (Genesis 1:27)

The Kingdom of God

The teachings of Jesus about the Kingdom of God present a vision of a just, peaceful, and reconciled world. The principles of restorative justice align with this vision, seeking to embody the values of the Kingdom in addressing harm and promoting healing.

1. Peace and Reconciliation: The Kingdom of God is characterized by peace, reconciliation, and justice. In Matthew 5:9, Jesus calls peacemakers blessed, highlighting the importance of fostering reconciliation and harmony.

Blessed are the peacemakers, for they shall be called sons of God. (Matthew 5:9)

2. Justice and Mercy: In the Beatitudes (Matthew 5:3-12), Jesus emphasizes qualities such as mercy, meekness, and

a hunger for righteousness. These qualities are integral to restorative justice, which seeks to balance justice with compassion and mercy.

Blessed are the merciful, for they shall receive mercy. (Matthew 5:7)

The Ministry of Reconciliation

The apostolic teachings on the ministry of reconciliation, particularly Paul's epistles, emphasize the call for believers to be agents of reconciliation. This ministry reflects the essence of restorative justice, focusing on restoring relationships with God and others.

Ambassadors for Christ: In 2 Corinthians 5:20, Paul describes believers as ambassadors for Christ, entrusted with the message of reconciliation. This role involves actively working to restore broken relationships and promote peace.

Therefore, we are ambassadors for Christ, God making his appeal through us. We implore you on behalf of Christ, to be reconciled to God. (2 Corinthians 5:20)

The biblical basis for restorative justice is robust and multifaceted, drawing from the laws of the Old Testament, the teachings of Jesus, and the apostolic writings. These scriptures emphasize the importance of restitution, reconciliation, and restoration, providing a theological foundation for the principles and practices of restorative justice.

As we continue to explore the teachings of Apostle Paul, we will see how his epistles further elucidate these principles and offer practical guidance for implementing restorative justice in our communities. Through this exploration, we aim to uncover timeless wisdom that can help us build a more just, compassionate, and restorative society.

OLD TESTAMENT EXAMPLES OF RESTORATIVE PRACTICES

The Old Testament is replete with examples of restorative practices that highlight the importance of repairing harm, restoring relationships, and ensuring justice in a way that upholds the dignity of all involved. These examples provide a rich foundation for understanding the principles of restorative justice and how they were applied in ancient Israelite society. This chapter delves into several key instances where restorative practices are evident, offering insights into their relevance and application.

Restitution for Theft and Property Damage

One of the most prominent examples of restorative justice in the Old Testament is the principle of restitution, particularly concerning theft and property damage.

Theft

In Exodus 22:1-4, the Law of Moses sets forth detailed instructions for restitution in cases of theft. The thief is required to repay multiple times the value of the stolen item, ensuring that the victim is adequately compensated for their loss.

When a man steals an ox or a sheep and slaughters it or sells it, he shall pay five oxen for the ox and four sheep for the sheep. If the stolen animal is found alive in his possession—whether ox or donkey or sheep—he shall pay back double. (Exodus 22:1-4)

This law emphasizes the offender's responsibility to make amends and restore what was taken, rather than focusing solely on punitive measures. The requirement to repay more than what was stolen serves as a deterrent while also ensuring that the victim's needs are met.

Property Damage

Leviticus 6:1-7 provides further guidelines for restitution, extending beyond theft to include various forms of property damage and dishonesty. The offender must not only return what was taken or damaged but also add a fifth of its value as compensation.

He shall restore it in full and add a fifth to it. He shall give it to the owner on the day he acknowledges his guilt. (Leviticus 6:5)

This additional compensation recognizes the broader impact of the harm and seeks to restore the relationship between the offender and the victim.

Cities of Refuge

The concept of cities of refuge, as described in Numbers 35:9-34, offers a profound example of restorative justice in action. These cities provided asylum for individuals who had committed unintentional manslaughter, protecting them from vengeance while ensuring that justice was served.

Purpose and Function

The cities of refuge were strategically located throughout Israel to be accessible to all. They served multiple purposes:

1. Protection from Avengers: The cities offered protection from the avenger of blood, who might seek to kill the offender in retaliation. This provision prevented cycles of vengeance and bloodshed, promoting a more measured approach to justice.

2. Fair Trial: Upon reaching a city of refuge, the offender was guaranteed a fair trial to determine whether the

killing was accidental or intentional. This process ensured that justice was based on a thorough examination of the facts.

3. Restoration: If found guilty of unintentional manslaughter, the offender was required to remain in the city of refuge until the death of the high priest, symbolizing a period of atonement and reflection. This period aimed at restoring the offender and allowing time for reconciliation with the victim's family.

The cities will serve as places of refuge from the avenger, so that anyone accused of murder may not die before they stand trial before the assembly. (Numbers 35:12)

Jubilee and the Year of Release

The concepts of Jubilee and the Year of Release, found in Leviticus 25 and Deuteronomy 15 respectively, illustrate systemic restorative practices designed to promote social and economic justice.

The Year of Jubilee

Every fiftieth year, the Israelites were to observe the Year of Jubilee, a time of liberation and restoration.

1. Release of Debts: All debts were to be forgiven, providing economic relief to those who had fallen into poverty or bondage. This practice prevented perpetual indebtedness and allowed individuals and families to start anew.

2. Restoration of Property: Land that had been sold due to economic hardship was to be returned to its original owners. This ensured that families could regain their ancestral inheritance, maintaining social stability and economic balance.

3. Freedom for Slaves: Hebrew slaves were to be set free, allowing them to return to their families and reclaim their freedom.

You shall proclaim liberty throughout the land to all its inhabitants. It shall be a jubilee for you when each of you shall return to his property and each of you shall return to his clan. (Leviticus 25:10)

The Year of Release

Every seventh year, the Israelites were to observe the Year of Release, which included the release of debts and the freeing of Hebrew slaves.

1. Debt Cancellation: All debts were to be forgiven, providing a fresh start for those burdened by financial obligations.

2. Compassion and Generosity: This practice encouraged a culture of compassion and generosity, reminding the Israelites of their own liberation from Egypt and their duty to care for one another.

At the end of every seven years you shall grant a release. And this is the manner of the release: every creditor shall release what he has lent to his neighbor. He shall not exact it of his neighbor, his brother, because the Lord's release has been proclaimed. (Deuteronomy 15:1-2)

Prophetic Calls for Restorative Justice

The prophets of the Old Testament frequently called for justice, mercy, and the restoration of relationships, reflecting the core principles of restorative justice.

Isaiah's Vision of Justice

Isaiah's prophetic ministry emphasized the need for social justice, compassion, and the restoration of the oppressed.

Learn to do good; seek justice, correct oppression; bring justice to the fatherless, plead the widow's cause. (Isaiah 1:17)

Isaiah's call to seek justice and correct oppression highlights the active role that individuals and communities must play in restoring justice and caring for the vulnerable.

Micah's Call for Justice and Mercy

Micah 6:8 encapsulates the essence of restorative justice, calling for justice, mercy, and humility.

He has told you, O man, what is good; and what does the Lord require of you but to do justice, and to love kindness, and to walk humbly with your God? (Micah 6:8)

Micah's message emphasizes that true justice involves not only legal and economic restitution but also compassionate and humble relationships.

Case Study: The Story of Joseph and His Brothers

The story of Joseph and his brothers in Genesis 37-50 provides a powerful narrative of restorative justice, reconciliation, and forgiveness.

The Harm

Joseph's brothers sold him into slavery out of jealousy, causing immense harm to Joseph and their family.

Then Midianite traders passed by, and they drew Joseph up and lifted him out of the pit, and sold him to the Ishmaelites for twenty shekels of silver. They took Joseph to Egypt. (Genesis 37:28)

The Restoration

Years later, when Joseph had risen to a position of power in Egypt, his brothers came to him seeking food during a famine. Instead of seeking revenge, Joseph chose to forgive them and restore their relationship.

1. Testing and Transformation: Joseph tested his brothers to see if they had changed. Their remorse and willingness to sacrifice for one another demonstrated their transformation.

2. Reconciliation: Joseph revealed his identity to his brothers, expressing forgiveness and a desire for reconciliation.

And now do not be distressed or angry with yourselves because you sold me here, for God sent me before you to preserve life. (Genesis 45:5)

3. Restoration of Relationship: Joseph's forgiveness led to the restoration of his family. He invited his entire family to live in Egypt, ensuring their well-being and preserving their future.

So Joseph settled his father and his brothers and gave them possession in the land of Egypt, in the best of the land, in the land of Rameses, as Pharaoh had commanded. (Genesis 47:11)

The Old Testament provides numerous examples of restorative practices that emphasize repairing harm, restoring relationships, and promoting justice. From the laws of restitution and the cities of refuge to the prophetic calls for justice and mercy, these practices highlight the importance of a justice system that seeks healing and reconciliation.

As we continue to explore the teachings of Apostle Paul, we will see how these Old Testament principles are echoed and expanded in the New Testament, offering a comprehensive framework for understanding and applying restorative justice in our lives and communities. Through this exploration, we aim to uncover timeless wisdom that can help us build a more just, compassionate, and restorative society.

JESUS' TEACHINGS ON FORGIVENESS AND RECONCILIATION

Jesus' teachings on forgiveness and reconciliation are foundational to the Christian faith and provide a profound framework for understanding restorative justice. Through parables, sermons, and interactions with individuals, Jesus emphasized the importance of forgiving others, seeking reconciliation, and restoring broken relationships. This chapter explores key teachings of Jesus that highlight these principles and their implications for restorative justice.

The Parable of the Prodigal Son

One of the most powerful illustrations of forgiveness and reconciliation is found in the Parable of the Prodigal Son (Luke 15:11-32). This parable encapsulates the themes of repentance, unconditional love, and the restoration of relationships.

The Story

In the parable, a younger son demands his inheritance from his father and then squanders it in reckless living. When he finds himself destitute, he decides to return home, repentant and hoping to be accepted back as a servant.

So, he got up and went to his father. But while he was still a long way off, his father saw him and was filled with compassion for him; he ran to his son, threw his arms around him, and kissed him. (Luke 15:20)

Key Themes

1. Unconditional Love: The father's willingness to forgive and restore his son without hesitation demonstrates unconditional love and grace. This mirrors God's love for humanity and His readiness to forgive those who repent.

2. Repentance and Humility: The younger son's return home signifies repentance and humility. Acknowledging his wrongs and seeking forgiveness are crucial steps in the process of reconciliation.

3. Restoration of Relationship: The father's actions not only forgive but also restore the son's status as a beloved member of the family. This restoration is central to the concept of reconciliation in restorative justice.

Teaching on Forgiveness

Jesus' teachings on forgiveness are clear and unequivocal, emphasizing the necessity of forgiving others as a reflection of God's forgiveness toward us.

Unlimited Forgiveness

In Matthew 18:21-22, Peter asks Jesus how many times he should forgive someone who sins against him, suggesting up to seven times. Jesus responds by expanding this number exponentially.

Jesus answered, "I tell you, not seven times, but seventy-seven times." (Matthew 18:22)

This statement underscores that forgiveness should not be limited or conditional. Instead, it should be a continuous practice, reflecting the boundless nature of God's forgiveness.

The Parable of the Unforgiving Servant

To illustrate the importance of forgiveness, Jesus tells the Parable of the Unforgiving Servant (Matthew 18:23-35). In this story, a servant who is forgiven an enormous debt by his master refuses to forgive a small debt owed to him by another servant.

Then the master called the servant in. 'You wicked servant,' he said, 'I canceled all that debt of yours because you begged me to. Shouldn't you have had mercy on your fellow servant just as I had on you?' (Matthew 18:32-33)

Key Lessons

1. Gratitude and Reciprocity: The parable highlights the expectation that those who have received forgiveness should extend the same grace to others. It teaches that

forgiveness is not only an act of mercy but also a reflection of gratitude for the forgiveness we have received.

2. Consequences of Unforgiveness: The servant's failure to forgive leads to severe consequences, illustrating that withholding forgiveness can perpetuate harm and hinder reconciliation.

Reconciliation with Others

Jesus taught that reconciliation should be a priority for those who seek to live according to God's will. This is evident in His instructions on addressing conflicts and seeking to restore broken relationships.

The Sermon on the Mount

In the Sermon on the Mount, Jesus emphasizes the importance of reconciling with others before offering gifts to God.

Therefore, if you are offering your gift at the altar and there remember that your brother or sister has something against you, leave your gift there in front of the altar. First go and be reconciled to them; then come and offer your gift. (Matthew 5:23-24)

Key Principles

1. Priority of Reconciliation: Jesus teaches that reconciliation with others takes precedence over religious

rituals. This underscores the importance of mending relationships as a fundamental aspect of spiritual life.

2. Proactive Effort: The instruction to seek reconciliation involves taking the initiative to address conflicts and make amends. This proactive effort is crucial in restorative justice, where the goal is to heal and restore relationships.

The Process of Addressing Conflicts

In Matthew 18:15-17, Jesus outlines a step-by-step process for addressing conflicts within the community, emphasizing restoration over punishment.

1. Private Correction: If someone sins against you, address the issue privately with the person. This approach respects the dignity of the individual and provides an opportunity for resolution without public shame.

If your brother or sister sins, go and point out their fault, just between the two of you. If they listen to you, you have won them over. (Matthew 18:15)

2. Involving Witnesses: If private correction fails, involve one or two others to help mediate and ensure a fair process.

But if they will not listen, take one or two others along, so that 'every matter may be established by the testimony of two or three witnesses.' (Matthew 18:16)

3. Bringing it to the Community: If the individual still refuses to listen, bring the matter before the community for resolution.

If they still refuse to listen, tell it to the church; and if they refuse to listen even to the church, treat them as you would a pagan or a tax collector. (Matthew 18:17)

This process emphasizes restoration and reconciliation, providing multiple opportunities for the offender to repent and make amends before any punitive action is considered.

Examples of Jesus Practicing Forgiveness and Reconciliation

Throughout His ministry, Jesus demonstrated forgiveness and reconciliation in His interactions with individuals, providing powerful examples for His followers.

The Adulterous Woman

In John 8:1-11, a woman caught in adultery is brought before Jesus by religious leaders seeking to stone her according to the law. Jesus responds by challenging those without sin to cast the first stone, ultimately forgiving the woman and instructing her to leave her life of sin.

Jesus straightened up and asked her, "Woman, where are they? Has no one condemned you?" "No one, sir," she said. "Then neither do I condemn you," Jesus declared. "Go now and leave your life of sin." (John 8:10-11)

Key Lessons

1. Compassion and Mercy: Jesus' response demonstrates compassion and mercy, focusing on the woman's potential for transformation rather than her punishment.

2. Encouragement to Change: While forgiving her, Jesus also encourages her to change her ways, highlighting the restorative goal of repentance and personal growth.

Zacchaeus the Tax Collector

In Luke 19:1-10, Jesus encounters Zacchaeus, a tax collector known for his dishonesty. Jesus invites Himself to Zacchaeus' home, leading to Zacchaeus' repentance and commitment to restitution.

But Zacchaeus stood up and said to the Lord, "Look, Lord! Here and now I give half of my possessions to the poor, and if I have cheated anybody out of anything, I will pay back four times the amount." (Luke 19:8)

Key Lessons

1. Restitution and Repentance: Zacchaeus' willingness to repay those he has wronged exemplifies the principles of restitution and repentance in restorative justice.

2. Acceptance and Transformation: Jesus' acceptance of Zacchaeus leads to his transformation, demonstrating the power of grace and inclusion in fostering change and reconciliation.

Jesus' teachings on forgiveness and reconciliation provide a comprehensive foundation for restorative justice. Through parables, sermons, and personal interactions, Jesus emphasized the importance of forgiving others, seeking reconciliation, and restoring broken relationships. These teachings align closely with the principles of restorative justice, which focus on healing, accountability, and the restoration of community harmony.

As we continue to explore the teachings of Apostle Paul, we will see how these principles are further developed and applied in his epistles, offering practical guidance for implementing restorative justice in our lives and communities. By embracing Jesus' teachings on forgiveness and reconciliation, we can build a more just, compassionate, and restorative society.

THE KINGDOM OF GOD AS A RESTORATIVE COMMUNITY

The Kingdom of God, as depicted in the teachings of Jesus, represents a vision of a just, peaceful, and restorative community. This chapter explores how the concept of the Kingdom of God aligns with the principles of restorative justice, emphasizing healing, reconciliation, and the restoration of relationships. By examining Jesus' teachings and actions, we will see how the Kingdom of God serves as a model for restorative practices within Christian communities.

The Vision of the Kingdom of God

Characteristics of the Kingdom

Jesus frequently spoke about the Kingdom of God, describing it as a realm where God's will is done on earth as it is in heaven. The Kingdom is characterized by:

1. Justice: The Kingdom of God promotes justice, where the needs of the oppressed and marginalized are addressed, and fairness prevails.

2. Peace: The Kingdom is a place of peace and harmony, where conflicts are resolved, and relationships are restored.

3. Love and Compassion: Love and compassion are central to the Kingdom, reflecting God's nature and guiding interactions among its members.

4. Inclusivity: The Kingdom is inclusive, welcoming people from all backgrounds and statuses, breaking down barriers of division.

The Lord's Prayer

The Lord's Prayer, taught by Jesus, encapsulates the vision of the Kingdom of God:

Our Father in heaven, hallowed be your name, your kingdom come, you will be done, on earth as it is in heaven. (Matthew 6:9-10)

This prayer reflects the desire for God's restorative justice to be manifested on earth, where His will is done through acts of mercy, forgiveness, and reconciliation.

Jesus' Teachings on the Kingdom of God

The Beatitudes

The Beatitudes, part of the Sermon on the Mount, describe the values and attitudes that characterize the Kingdom of God (Matthew 5:3-12). These values align closely with restorative justice principles.

Blessed are the peacemakers, for they will be called children of God. (Matthew 5:9)

Key Values

1. Mercy: The Beatitudes emphasize mercy, highlighting the importance of compassionate responses to wrongdoing.

Blessed are the merciful, for they will be shown mercy. (Matthew 5:7)

2. Peacemaking: Peacemakers are honored in the Kingdom, reflecting the priority of resolving conflicts and restoring harmony.

3. Hunger for Righteousness: A commitment to righteousness and justice is a defining feature of the Kingdom.

Blessed are those who hunger and thirst for righteousness, for they will be filled. (Matthew 5:6)

Parables Illustrating Restorative Justice in the Kingdom

Jesus used parables to illustrate the principles of the Kingdom of God, many of which highlight restorative justice themes.

The Parable of the Lost Sheep

In Luke 15:3-7, Jesus tells the parable of the lost sheep, where a shepherd leaves ninety-nine sheep to find one that is lost. This parable emphasizes the value of every individual and the lengths to which God will go to restore those who are lost.

And when he finds it, he joyfully puts it on his shoulders and goes home. Then he calls his friends and neighbors together and says, 'Rejoice with me; I have found my lost sheep.' (Luke 15:5-6)

Key Lessons

1. Individual Worth: Every person is valuable in the eyes of God, deserving of effort and care to bring them back into the fold.

2. Restoration and Joy: The restoration of the lost sheep brings joy to the community, reflecting the communal aspect of restorative justice.

The Parable of the Good Samaritan

In Luke 10:25-37, Jesus tells the parable of the Good Samaritan, where a Samaritan helps a man who has been beaten and left for dead, while others pass by. This parable highlights the importance of compassion and action in the face of suffering.

But a Samaritan, as he traveled, came where the man was; and when he saw him, he took pity on him. (Luke 10:33)

Key Lessons

1. Compassionate Action: True neighborliness involves active compassion and assistance, not just sympathy.

2. Breaking Barriers: The Samaritan's actions break social and ethnic barriers, reflecting the inclusivity of the Kingdom.

Jesus' Actions as Examples of Restorative Practices

Healing and Restoration

Jesus' ministry was marked by acts of healing and restoration, which serve as examples of restorative justice.

1. Healing the Blind and Lame: Jesus often healed those who were blind, lame, or suffering from various ailments, restoring them to full participation in the community.

Jesus went through all the towns and villages, teaching in their synagogues, proclaiming the good news of the kingdom, and healing every disease and sickness. (Matthew 9:35)

2. Raising the Dead: Jesus raised individuals from the dead, restoring them to their families and communities, exemplifying the ultimate act of restoration.

Jesus said to her, "I am the resurrection and the life. The one who believes in me will live, even though they die." (John 11:25)

Forgiveness and Inclusion

Jesus' interactions with marginalized individuals demonstrate the restorative nature of the Kingdom.

1. The Woman Caught in Adultery: In John 8:1-11, Jesus forgives a woman caught in adultery and challenges her accusers, emphasizing forgiveness over condemnation.

Then neither do I condemn you," Jesus declared. "Go now and leave your life of sin. (John 8:11)

2. Zacchaeus the Tax Collector: In Luke 19:1-10, Jesus invites Himself to the house of Zacchaeus, a despised tax collector, leading to Zacchaeus' repentance and restitution.

But Zacchaeus stood up and said to the Lord, "Look, Lord! Here and now I give half of my possessions to the poor, and if I have cheated anybody out of anything, I will pay back four times the amount." (Luke 19:8)

The Church as a Restorative Community

The Early Church Model

The early Christian community modeled the principles of the Kingdom of God, focusing on communal living, mutual support, and restorative practices.

1. Sharing Resources: Acts 2:44-45 describes the early believers sharing their possessions and resources to ensure that no one was in need.

All the believers were together and had everything in common. They sold property and possessions to give to anyone who had need. (Acts 2:44-45)

2. Addressing Conflicts: The early church practiced restorative discipline, aiming to correct and restore rather than punish.

If your brother or sister sins against you, go and point out their fault, just between the two of you. If they listen to you, you have won them over. (Matthew 18:15)

Modern Applications

1. Community Support Systems: Churches today can create support systems for those who have been harmed or have caused harm, facilitating healing and reconciliation.

2. Restorative Programs: Implementing restorative justice programs, such as victim-offender mediation and restorative circles, within church communities can promote healing and restoration.

The Kingdom of God, as depicted in Jesus' teachings and actions, serves as a model for a restorative community. Its principles of justice, peace, love, compassion, and inclusivity align closely with restorative justice, providing a vision for how Christian communities can embody these values.

As we continue to explore the teachings of Apostle Paul, we will see how he further develops these principles, offering practical guidance for implementing restorative justice in our lives and communities. By striving to reflect the Kingdom of God, we can build a more just, compassionate, and restorative society, grounded in the teachings and example of Jesus.

CHAPTER 03

APOSTLE PAUL'S BACKGROUND AND CONVERSION

Paul's Early Life and Background

To fully understand the profound impact of Apostle Paul's teachings on restorative justice, it is essential to examine his early life and background. Paul's journey from a zealous persecutor of Christians to a devoted apostle of Jesus Christ provides valuable insights into the transformative power of grace and the principles of reconciliation and restoration that underpin his teachings.

Early Life and Education

Birth and Heritage

Paul, originally named Saul, was born in Tarsus, a major city in the Roman province of Cilicia (modern-day Turkey). Tarsus was known for its cultural and intellectual significance, which likely influenced Paul's early development.

1. Jewish Heritage: Paul was born to Jewish parents and belonged to the tribe of Benjamin. He was a Roman citizen by birth, a status that afforded him certain legal protections and privileges.

I am a Jew, from Tarsus in Cilicia, a citizen of no ordinary city. (Acts 21:39)

2. Roman Citizenship: Paul's Roman citizenship played a crucial role in his missionary journeys, providing him with opportunities to travel freely and appeal to Roman authorities when necessary.

But Paul said to the centurion standing there, "Is it legal for you to flog a Roman citizen who hasn't even been found guilty?" (Acts 22:25)

Education and Training

Paul received an extensive education in both Jewish law and Greek culture, which equipped him with the knowledge and skills necessary for his later missionary work.

1. Training under Gamaliel: Paul was trained in Jerusalem under the renowned Rabbi Gamaliel, a leading authority in the Jewish Sanhedrin. This rigorous education grounded him in the Hebrew Scriptures and Jewish traditions.

I am a Jew, born in Tarsus of Cilicia, but brought up in this city. I studied under Gamaliel and was thoroughly trained in the law of our ancestors. (Acts 22:3)

2. Knowledge of Greek Culture: Growing up in Tarsus, Paul was exposed to Greek philosophy, rhetoric, and culture. This exposure enabled him to effectively communicate the gospel to diverse audiences throughout the Roman Empire.

Zealous Persecution of Christians

Before his dramatic conversion, Paul was known for his zealous persecution of Christians. His actions were motivated by his deep commitment to Jewish law and his belief that the followers of Jesus were a threat to the Jewish faith.

Role in Stephen's Martyrdom

Paul's involvement in the persecution of Christians is most notably marked by his presence at the stoning of Stephen, the first Christian martyr.

1. Approval of Stephen's Death: Paul, then known as Saul, approved of Stephen's execution and actively participated in the efforts to eradicate the early Christian movement.

And Saul approved of their killing him. On that day a great persecution broke out against the church in Jerusalem, and all except the apostles were scattered throughout Judea and Samaria. (Acts 8:1)

2. Guarding the Coats: Saul held the coats of those who stoned Stephen, indicating his active support for the execution.

Meanwhile, the witnesses laid their coats at the feet of a young man named Saul. (Acts 7:58)

Persecution of the Church

Paul's zeal for Jewish law led him to persecute Christians with fervor, believing he was protecting the purity of the Jewish faith.

1. Arresting Christians: Paul sought to arrest and imprison Christians, targeting both men and women who followed "the Way" (early Christianity).

But Saul began to destroy the church. Going from house to house, he dragged off both men and women and put them in prison. (Acts 8:3)

2. Authority from the High Priest: Paul received authority from the High Priest to pursue Christians even beyond Jerusalem, highlighting his determination to eradicate the new faith.

I persecuted the followers of this Way to their death, arresting both men and women and throwing them into prison, as the high priest and all the Council can themselves testify. (Acts 22:4-5)

The Damascus Road Experience

Paul's dramatic conversion on the road to Damascus marks a turning point in his life, transforming him from a persecutor of Christians to one of the most influential apostles of Jesus Christ.

The Encounter with Jesus

While traveling to Damascus to arrest more Christians, Paul had a life-changing encounter with the risen Jesus.

1. The Blinding Light: A bright light from heaven suddenly shone around Paul, causing him to fall to the ground. This supernatural encounter initiated his conversion.

As he neared Damascus on his journey, suddenly a light from heaven flashed around him. He fell to the ground and heard a voice say to him, "Saul, Saul, why do you persecute me?" (Acts 9:3-4)

2. The Voice of Jesus: Jesus spoke to Paul, revealing Himself as the one Paul was persecuting. This direct confrontation led Paul to recognize Jesus as the Messiah.

"Who are you, Lord?" Saul asked. "I am Jesus, whom you are persecuting," he replied. (Acts 9:5)

Blindness and Reflection

Following the encounter, Paul was struck blind and led by his companions into Damascus. His physical blindness symbolized his spiritual blindness, and this period of darkness allowed him to reflect on his actions and beliefs.

For three days he was blind and did not eat or drink anything. (Acts 9:9)

Ananias' Role

God instructed a disciple named Ananias to visit Paul, heal his blindness, and baptize him. Ananias was initially hesitant due to Paul's reputation, but he obeyed God's command.

1. Healing and Baptism: Ananias laid hands on Paul, and his sight was restored. Paul was then baptized, marking his formal acceptance into the Christian faith.

Placing his hands on Saul, he said, "Brother Saul, the Lord—Jesus, who appeared to you on the road as you were coming here—has sent me so that you may see again and be filled with the Holy Spirit." Immediately, something like scales fell from Saul's eyes, and he could see again. He got up and was baptized. (Acts 9:17-18)

2. Commissioning: Ananias conveyed God's message that Paul was chosen to be a vessel to carry the gospel to the Gentiles, kings, and the people of Israel.

But the Lord said to Ananias, "Go! This man is my chosen instrument to proclaim my name to the Gentiles and their kings and to the people of Israel. (Acts 9:15)

Transformation and Mission

Paul's conversion was not just a personal transformation but also a commissioning for a new mission. He went from persecuting Christians to becoming a fervent apostle, spreading the message of Jesus Christ throughout the Roman Empire.

Immediate Preaching

After his conversion, Paul immediately began to preach about Jesus in the synagogues, proclaiming Him as the Son of God.

At once he began to preach in the synagogues that Jesus is the Son of God. (Acts 9:20)

Time in Arabia and Damascus

Paul spent time in Arabia and then returned to Damascus, where he continued to grow in his understanding of the gospel and his role as an apostle.

I did not go up to Jerusalem to see those who were apostles before I was, but I went into Arabia. Later I returned to Damascus. (Galatians 1:17)

Reconciliation with the Church

Initially, the Christian community was wary of Paul due to his past actions. However, Barnabas vouched for him, helping to integrate him into the community and establish his credibility as a true follower of Christ.

But Barnabas took him and brought him to the apostles. He told them how Saul on his journey had seen the Lord and that the Lord had spoken to him, and how in Damascus he had preached fearlessly in the name of Jesus. (Acts 9:27)

Theological Implications of Paul's Conversion

Paul's conversion experience profoundly shaped his theology and his approach to ministry. His teachings on grace, forgiveness, and reconciliation are deeply influenced by his own encounter with Jesus and the radical transformation he experienced.

Grace and Forgiveness

Paul's writings emphasize the unmerited grace of God and the importance of forgiveness. He often reflected on his past as a persecutor and the overwhelming grace he received from God.

Here is a trustworthy saying that deserves full acceptance: Christ Jesus came into the world to save sinners—of whom I am the worst. (1 Timothy 1:15)

Reconciliation

Paul's conversion also informed his teachings on reconciliation, both with God and within the community. He emphasized the ministry of reconciliation, urging believers to restore relationships and live in harmony.

All this is from God, who reconciled us to himself through Christ and gave us the ministry of reconciliation. (2 Corinthians 5:18)

Apostle Paul's early life and dramatic conversion provide a powerful narrative of transformation and redemption. From a zealous persecutor of Christians to a devoted apostle, Paul's journey exemplifies the principles of grace, forgiveness, and reconciliation that are central to restorative justice. His background and experiences deeply influenced his teachings, which continue to offer valuable insights for building a just, compassionate, and restorative community.

As we explore Paul's teachings further in this book, we will see how his understanding of restorative justice principles shaped his approach to ministry and his guidance for Christian communities. Through his life and writings

THE DAMASCUS ROAD EXPERIENCE AND ITS IMPACT

The Damascus Road experience marks a pivotal moment in the life of Apostle Paul, transforming him from a zealous persecutor of Christians into one of the most influential apostles of Jesus Christ. This chapter explores the details of this dramatic encounter, its immediate aftermath, and its profound impact on Paul's life and ministry. Understanding this transformative event is essential to grasp the depth of Paul's teachings on grace, reconciliation, and restorative justice.

The Damascus Road Encounter

The Journey to Damascus

Paul, then known as Saul, was on a mission to arrest Christians in Damascus and bring them back to Jerusalem for punishment. Armed with letters of authority from the high priest, he was determined to eradicate the fledgling Christian movement.

Meanwhile, Saul was still breathing out murderous threats against the Lord's disciples. He went to the high priest and asked him for letters to the synagogues in Damascus so that if he found any there who belonged to the Way, whether men or women, he might take them as prisoners to Jerusalem. (Acts 9:1-2)

The Divine Encounter

As Saul neared Damascus, a sudden, intense light from heaven flashed around him, causing him to fall to the ground. This supernatural event marked the beginning of his conversion.

1. The Blinding Light: The light was so bright that it temporarily blinded Saul, symbolizing both physical and spiritual blindness.

As he neared Damascus on his journey, suddenly a light from heaven flashed around him. He fell to the ground and heard a voice say to him, "Saul, Saul, why do you persecute me?" (Acts 9:3-4)

2. The Voice of Jesus: Jesus spoke directly to Saul, questioning his persecution of Christians and revealing His identity. This direct encounter with the risen Christ fundamentally challenged Saul's beliefs and actions.

"Who are you, Lord?" Saul asked. "I am Jesus, whom you are persecuting," he replied. (Acts 9:5)

Saul's Response

Confounded and blinded by the experience, Saul was led by his companions into Damascus. For three days, he remained blind, fasting and praying, reflecting on the profound implications of his encounter.

Saul got up from the ground, but when he opened his eyes he could see nothing. So they led him by the hand into Damascus. For three days he was blind and did not eat or drink anything. (Acts 9:8-9)

The Role of Ananias

God's Instruction to Ananias

God spoke to a disciple named Ananias in Damascus, instructing him to visit Saul, heal his blindness, and baptize him. Ananias was initially hesitant, aware of Saul's reputation as a persecutor of Christians, but he obeyed God's command.

1. Divine Mandate: God reassured Ananias of Saul's chosen role in spreading the gospel.

But the Lord said to Ananias, "Go! This man is my chosen instrument to proclaim my name to the Gentiles and their kings and to the people of Israel. (Acts 9:15)

2. Healing and Baptism: Ananias laid hands on Saul, restoring his sight and baptizing him. This act signified Saul's acceptance into the Christian community and his commitment to his new faith.

Then Ananias went to the house and entered it. Placing his hands on Saul, he said, "Brother Saul, the Lord—Jesus, who appeared to you on the road as you were coming here—has sent me so that you may see again and be filled with the Holy Spirit." Immediately, something like scales fell from Saul's eyes, and he could see again. He got up and was baptized. (Acts 9:17-18)

Immediate Aftermath and Transformation

Preaching in Damascus

Following his conversion, Saul, now known as Paul, began to preach about Jesus in the synagogues of Damascus, proclaiming Him as the Son of God. This radical transformation from persecutor to proponent shocked many who knew of his former zeal against Christians.

At once he began to preach in the synagogues that Jesus is the Son of God. All those who heard him were astonished and asked, "Isn't he the man who raised havoc in Jerusalem among those who call on this name? And hasn't he come here to take them as prisoners to the chief priests?" (Acts 9:20-21)

Opposition and Escape

Paul's bold preaching soon aroused opposition from the Jewish leaders in Damascus, who plotted to kill him. However, his new Christian friends helped him escape the city by lowering him in a basket through an opening in the city wall.

But his followers took him by night and lowered him in a basket through an opening in the wall. (Acts 9:25)

Long-Term Impact on Paul's Ministry

Theological Development

The Damascus Road experience profoundly influenced Paul's theological perspective, particularly his understanding of grace, redemption, and the inclusion of Gentiles in God's plan of salvation.

1. Grace and Mercy: Paul's dramatic conversion underscored the unmerited grace and mercy of God. Despite his past as a persecutor, Paul received forgiveness and a new mission, which he frequently emphasized in his writings.

But for that very reason I was shown mercy so that in me, the worst of sinners, Christ Jesus might display his immense patience as an example for those who would believe in him and receive eternal life. (1 Timothy 1:16)

2. Universal Mission: Paul's calling to be the apostle to the Gentiles expanded the scope of the gospel beyond the Jewish community, emphasizing the inclusivity and universality of God's love and salvation.

It was to reveal his Son in me so that I might preach him among the Gentiles. (Galatians 1:16)

Advocacy for Reconciliation

Paul's teachings on reconciliation reflect the restorative nature of his own conversion experience. He often wrote about the importance of reconciling with God and with one another, promoting peace and unity within the Christian community.

1. Reconciliation with God: Paul emphasized that through Jesus Christ, humanity is reconciled to God, receiving forgiveness and restoration.

All this is from God, who reconciled us to Himself through Christ and gave us the ministry of reconciliation. (2 Corinthians 5:18)

2. Reconciliation within the Community: Paul also taught that believers should seek reconciliation with each other, resolving conflicts and restoring relationships.

If it is possible, as far as it depends on you, live at peace with everyone. (Romans 12:18)

The Damascus Road Experience as a Model of Restorative Justice

Transformation and Restoration

Paul's conversion is a powerful example of transformation and restoration, core principles of restorative justice. His encounter with Jesus not only changed his life but also restored him to a new purpose and mission.

1. Personal Transformation: Paul's life was radically transformed from one of violence and persecution to one of preaching and reconciliation.

2. Restored Purpose: Paul's new mission to spread the gospel and build up the Christian community reflects the restorative aspect of his conversion.

Forgiveness and New Identity

The forgiveness Paul received on the Damascus Road highlights the restorative justice principle of offering a new identity and future to those who have caused harm.

1. Forgiveness: Despite his past, Paul was forgiven and given a new start, demonstrating the power of God's grace and mercy.

2. New Identity: Paul's new identity as an apostle of Christ underscores the idea that restorative justice seeks to transform and rehabilitate rather than simply punish.

The Damascus Road experience was a watershed moment in Paul's life, setting the course for his future ministry and shaping his theological perspectives. This encounter with the risen Jesus not only transformed Paul but also underscored the principles of grace, forgiveness, and reconciliation that are central to restorative justice.

As we continue to explore Paul's teachings, we will see how his own experience of radical transformation and restorative grace informs his writings and offers practical guidance for building a just and compassionate community. Through his example and teachings, we can gain a deeper understanding of how to embody the principles of restorative justice in our lives and communities.

THE TRANSFORMATION FROM PERSECUTOR TO APOSTLE

Apostle Paul's transformation from a zealous persecutor of Christians to one of the most influential apostles of Jesus Christ is one of the most remarkable stories of conversion and redemption in Christian history. This chapter explores the profound change in Paul's life, the factors that contributed to his transformation, and the impact of his new identity on his mission and teachings.

Early Life as a Persecutor

Saul's Zeal for Jewish Law

Before his conversion, Saul (Paul's original name) was a fervent adherent of Jewish law and traditions. His education under Rabbi Gamaliel, a respected teacher in the Jewish Sanhedrin, grounded him deeply in the Pharisaic traditions and zealousness for the purity of the Jewish faith.

1. Devotion to the Law: Saul's rigorous training made him passionate about upholding Jewish law and opposing any movement that threatened its integrity, including the nascent Christian faith.

I was advancing in Judaism beyond many of my own age among my people and was extremely zealous for the traditions of my fathers. (Galatians 1:14)

2. Persecution of Christians: Saul viewed the followers of Jesus, referred to as "the Way," as a dangerous sect that needed to be eradicated. He sought to arrest and imprison Christians, believing he was protecting the Jewish faith.

But Saul began to destroy the church. Going from house to house, he dragged off both men and women and put them in prison. (Acts 8:3)

The Stoning of Stephen

Saul's involvement in the persecution of Christians is vividly illustrated in his participation in the stoning of Stephen, the first Christian martyr.

1. Approval of Execution: Saul not only approved of Stephen's execution but also actively supported it by guarding the clothes of those who stoned Stephen.

And Saul approved of their killing him. (Acts 8:1)

2. Witness to Persecution: This event marked Saul as a key figure in the early persecution of Christians, reflecting his deep commitment to his cause.

Meanwhile, the witnesses laid their coats at the feet of a young man named Saul. (Acts 7:58)

The Damascus Road Experience

The Encounter with Christ

Saul's life took a dramatic turn on the road to Damascus, where he intended to arrest Christians and bring them to Jerusalem. His encounter with the risen Jesus profoundly changed his trajectory.

1. Blinding Light and Voice: As Saul neared Damascus, a brilliant light from heaven suddenly surrounded him, and he fell to the ground. He heard a voice saying, "Saul, Saul, why do you persecute me?"

As he neared Damascus on his journey, suddenly a light from heaven flashed around him. He fell to the ground and heard a voice say to him, "Saul, Saul, why do you persecute me?" (Acts 9:3-4)

2. Identification of Jesus: When Saul asked who was speaking, Jesus revealed Himself, saying, "I am Jesus, whom you are persecuting." This revelation confronted Saul with the reality that his persecution of Christians was, in fact, an attack on Jesus Himself.

"Who are you, Lord?" Saul asked. "I am Jesus, whom you are persecuting," he replied. (Acts 9:5)

Saul's Blindness and Reflection

Following the encounter, Saul was struck blind and had to be led into Damascus by his companions. For three days, he remained blind, fasting and praying, deeply reflecting on the encounter and its implications.

For three days he was blind and did not eat or drink anything. (Acts 9:9)

Ananias' Role in Saul's Transformation

God instructed a disciple named Ananias to visit Saul, heal his blindness, and baptize him. Despite his initial fear due to Saul's reputation, Ananias obeyed God's command.

1. Healing and Baptism: Ananias laid hands on Saul, restored his sight, and baptized him, marking his formal acceptance into the Christian faith.

Then Ananias went to the house and entered it. Placing his hands on Saul, he said, "Brother Saul, the Lord—Jesus, who appeared to you on the road as you were coming here—has sent me so that you may see again and be filled with the Holy Spirit." Immediately, something like scales fell from Saul's eyes, and he could see again. He got up and was baptized. (Acts 9:17-18)

2. Commissioning: Ananias conveyed God's message that Saul was chosen to be a vessel to carry the gospel to the Gentiles, kings, and the people of Israel.

But the Lord said to Ananias, "Go! This man is my chosen instrument to proclaim my name to the Gentiles and their kings and to the people of Israel. (Acts 9:15)

Transformation and New Identity

Immediate Preaching

After his conversion, Saul, now called Paul, began to preach about Jesus in the synagogues of Damascus, proclaiming Him as the Son of God. This immediate shift from persecutor to preacher astonished many who knew of his previous zeal against Christians.

At once he began to preach in the synagogues that Jesus is the Son of God. All those who heard him were astonished and asked, "Isn't he the man who raised havoc in Jerusalem among those who call on this name? And hasn't he come here to take them as prisoners to the chief priests?" (Acts 9:20-21)

Escape from Damascus

Paul's bold preaching soon aroused opposition from the Jewish leaders in Damascus, who plotted to kill him. With the help of his new Christian friends, Paul escaped the city by being lowered in a basket through an opening in the wall.

But his followers took him by night and lowered him in a basket through an opening in the wall. (Acts 9:25)

Integration into the Christian Community

Initially, the Christian community was wary of Paul due to his past actions. However, Barnabas, a respected Christian leader, vouched for him, helping to integrate him into the community and establish his credibility as a true follower of Christ.

But Barnabas took him and brought him to the apostles. He told them how Saul on his journey had seen the Lord and that the Lord had spoken to him, and how in Damascus he had preached fearlessly in the name of Jesus. (Acts 9:27)

Impact on Paul's Ministry

Mission to the Gentiles

Paul's calling as the apostle to the Gentiles expanded the scope of the gospel beyond the Jewish community, emphasizing the inclusivity and universality of God's love and salvation.

1. Preaching to the Gentiles: Paul's mission focused on spreading the gospel to non-Jewish populations, and breaking down cultural and religious barriers.

It was to reveal his Son in me so that I might preach him among the Gentiles. (Galatians 1:16)

2. Church Planting: Paul established numerous churches throughout the Roman Empire, nurturing diverse communities of believers and addressing their unique challenges.

Theological Contributions

Paul's theological insights, deeply influenced by his conversion experience, shaped the early Christian church and continue to impact Christian thought today.

1. Grace and Justification: Paul emphasized that salvation is a gift of grace through faith in Jesus Christ, not through adherence to the law. His writings on justification by faith are foundational to Christian theology.

For it is by grace you have been saved, through faith— and this is not from yourselves, it is the gift of God. (Ephesians 2:8)

2. Unity in Christ: Paul taught that in Christ, there is no distinction between Jew and Gentile, slave and free, male and female. All are one in Christ, reflecting the inclusive nature of the gospel.

There is neither Jew nor Gentile, neither slave nor free, nor is there male and female, for you are all one in Christ Jesus. (Galatians 3:28)

Advocacy for Restorative Justice

Paul's teachings on reconciliation and restoration reflect the transformative nature of his own conversion experience. He frequently wrote about the importance of restoring broken relationships, both with God and within the community.

1. Reconciliation with God: Paul emphasized that through Jesus Christ, humanity is reconciled to God, receiving forgiveness and restoration.

All this is from God, who reconciled us to Himself through Christ and gave us the ministry of reconciliation. (2 Corinthians 5:18)

2. Restoration within the Community: Paul also taught that believers should seek reconciliation with each other, promoting peace and unity within the Christian community.

If it is possible, as far as it depends on you, live at peace with everyone. (Romans 12:18)

Paul's transformation from a persecutor of Christians to a devoted apostle of Jesus Christ is a powerful testament to the transformative power of grace and the principles of restorative justice. His dramatic conversion on the Damascus Road not only changed the course of his life but also had a profound impact on his teachings and mission.

As we continue to explore Paul's writings, we will see how his understanding of grace, forgiveness, and reconciliation informs his approach to building a just and compassionate community. Through his life and teachings, we gain valuable insights into how to embody the principles of restorative justice in our own lives and communities, reflecting the transformative power of God's love and grace.

HOW PAUL'S CONVERSION REFLECTS RESTORATIVE PRINCIPLES

The conversion of Apostle Paul, from a vehement persecutor of Christians to a devoted apostle, is not only a testament to the transformative power of divine grace but also a vivid illustration of restorative principles at work. This chapter explores how Paul's conversion embodies the core tenets of restorative justice: accountability, forgiveness, transformation, and reconciliation.

The Encounter on the Damascus Road

Divine Intervention and Accountability

Paul's (then Saul) encounter with Jesus on the road to Damascus serves as a divine intervention that holds him accountable for his actions against Christians.

1. Recognition of Harm: Jesus' question, "Saul, Saul, why do you persecute me?" immediately confronts Paul with the reality of the harm he has been causing. This moment of accountability is crucial in restorative justice, where offenders must acknowledge the impact of their actions.

He fell to the ground and heard a voice say to him, "Saul, Saul, why do you persecute me?" (Acts 9:4)

2. Personal Responsibility: The encounter forces Paul to take personal responsibility for his persecution of Christians, as Jesus directly identifies Himself as the one being persecuted through His followers.

"Who are you, Lord?" Saul asked. "I am Jesus, whom you are persecuting," he replied. (Acts 9:5)

Blindness and Reflection

The immediate physical blindness that Paul experiences symbolizes his spiritual blindness and provides a period of reflection and penance.

1. Symbolic Blindness: Paul's blindness represents the need for introspection and spiritual awakening. This period of vulnerability allows him to contemplate his actions and their consequences.

Saul got up from the ground, but when he opened his eyes he could see nothing. So they led him by the hand into Damascus. (Acts 9:8)

2. Time for Reflection: The three days of blindness, during which Paul fasts and prays, are critical for his transformation. This time mirrors the restorative process where offenders reflect on their actions and begin the journey towards making amends.

For three days he was blind and did not eat or drink anything. (Acts 9:9)

The Role of Ananias: Forgiveness and Restoration

Ananias' Reluctance and Obedience

Ananias, a disciple in Damascus, plays a pivotal role in Paul's restoration, despite his initial fear and hesitation due to Paul's reputation.

1. Reluctance to Forgive: Ananias' reluctance highlights the natural human hesitation to forgive those who have caused significant harm. His obedience to God's command reflects the restorative principle of overcoming personal grievances to facilitate healing.

Lord," Ananias answered, "I have heard many reports about this man and all the harm he has done to your holy people in Jerusalem. (Acts 9:13)

2. Obedience and Acceptance: By obeying God and visiting Paul, Ananias embodies the restorative principle of extending forgiveness and facilitating the reintegration of the offender into the community.

Then Ananias went to the house and entered it. Placing his hands on Saul, he said, "Brother Saul, the Lord—Jesus, who appeared to you on the road as you were coming here—has sent me so that you may see again and be filled with the Holy Spirit." (Acts 9:17)

Healing and Baptism

Ananias' actions lead to Paul's physical and spiritual restoration, symbolized by the healing of his blindness and his subsequent baptism.

1. Physical Healing: The restoration of Paul's sight represents the removal of his spiritual blindness and his newfound clarity in understanding Jesus' message.

Immediately, something like scales fell from Saul's eyes, and he could see again. (Acts 9:18)

2. Spiritual Rebirth: Paul's baptism signifies his acceptance into the Christian community and his commitment to a new way of life, embodying the restorative principle of transformation and new beginnings.

He got up and was baptized. (Acts 9:18)

Transformation and New Mission

Immediate Preaching and Advocacy

Paul's immediate shift from persecutor to preacher demonstrates the transformative power of restorative justice, which seeks to rehabilitate and reintegrate offenders into society.

1. Transformation in Action: Paul begins to preach about Jesus in the synagogues of Damascus, proclaiming Him as the Son of God. This radical change highlights the potential for personal transformation when grace and forgiveness are extended.

At once he began to preach in the synagogues that Jesus is the Son of God. (Acts 9:20)

2. Advocacy for Reconciliation: Paul's teachings emphasize reconciliation with God and others, reflecting his own experience of being reconciled to the Christian community and to God through Jesus.

All this is from God, who reconciled us to Himself through Christ and gave us the ministry of reconciliation. (2 Corinthians 5:18)

Building Community and Inclusion

Paul's ministry focuses on building inclusive communities that embody the values of the Kingdom of God, emphasizing unity and reconciliation.

1. Inclusivity: Paul advocates for the inclusion of Gentiles into the Christian community, breaking down the barriers that previously divided Jews and Gentiles. This inclusivity reflects the restorative principle of healing fractured relationships and building a united community.

There is neither Jew nor Gentile, neither slave nor free, nor is there male and female, for you are all one in Christ Jesus. (Galatians 3:28)

2. Restorative Practices: Paul's letters often address conflicts within the early Christian communities, urging

believers to seek reconciliation and restore broken relationships.

If it is possible, as far as it depends on you, live at peace with everyone. (Romans 12:18)

Paul's Theological Reflections on Restoration

Grace and Justification

Paul's writings extensively discuss the themes of grace and justification, emphasizing that salvation is a gift from God, not earned by works but received through faith in Jesus Christ.

1. Unmerited Grace: Paul's own experience of receiving grace despite his past persecution of Christians underscores the restorative principle that everyone is capable of transformation and redemption.

For it is by grace you have been saved, through faith— and this is not from yourselves, it is the gift of God. (Ephesians 2:8)

2. Justification by Faith: Paul teaches that believers are justified by faith, not by adherence to the law. This doctrine highlights the transformative power of faith and the new identity that believers receive in Christ.

Therefore, since we have been justified through faith, we have peace with God through our Lord Jesus Christ. (Romans 5:1)

Reconciliation with God and Others

Paul's theology emphasizes the reconciliation of humanity with God through Jesus Christ, as well as the importance of reconciliation within the community.

1. Reconciliation with God: Paul teaches that through Christ's sacrificial death and resurrection, believers are reconciled to God, receiving forgiveness and a restored relationship with Him.

All this is from God, who reconciled us to Himself through Christ and gave us the ministry of reconciliation. (2 Corinthians 5:18)

2. Community Reconciliation: Paul encourages believers to forgive one another and seek reconciliation, fostering a community characterized by peace and unity.

Bear with each other and forgive one another if any of you has a grievance against someone. Forgive as the Lord forgave you. (Colossians 3:13)

Paul's conversion on the road to Damascus is a profound illustration of restorative principles in action. His journey from persecutor to apostle embodies the core tenets of restorative justice: accountability, forgiveness, transformation, and reconciliation. Paul's experience of divine grace and his subsequent mission to preach the gospel and build inclusive communities highlight the transformative power of forgiveness and the potential for personal and communal restoration.

As we delve deeper into Paul's teachings, we will continue to see how his understanding of grace, reconciliation, and restorative justice shapes his guidance for Christian communities. Through his life and writings, we gain valuable insights into how to apply restorative principles in our own lives, fostering healing, reconciliation, and unity in our communities.

CHAPTER 04

PAUL'S TEACHINGS ON FORGIVENESS AND RECONCILIATION

Apostle Paul's teachings on forgiveness and reconciliation form a cornerstone of his theological contributions and practical guidance for the early Christian communities. Through his letters, Paul provides profound insights into the nature of forgiveness, the necessity of reconciliation, and the ways in which believers can embody these principles in their lives. This chapter analyzes key passages from Paul's epistles, such as Romans 12:17-21 and 2 Corinthians 5:18-21, to understand his teachings on these essential Christian practices.

Romans 12:17-21: Overcoming Evil with Good

Context and Overview

In Romans 12, Paul outlines practical instructions for Christian living, emphasizing love, humility, and harmony within the community. Verses 17-21 specifically address how believers should respond to wrongdoing and conflict, promoting a restorative approach.

Do not repay anyone evil for evil. Be careful to do what is right in the eyes of everyone. If it is possible, as far as it depends on you, live at peace with everyone. Do not take revenge, my dear friends, but leave room for God's wrath, for it is written: "It is mine to avenge; I will repay," says the Lord. On the contrary: "If your enemy is hungry, feed him; if he is thirsty, give him something to drink. In doing this, you will heap burning coals on his head." Do not be overcome by evil, but overcome evil with good. (Romans 12:17-21)

Key Themes

1. Non-Retaliation: Paul explicitly instructs believers not to repay evil with evil. Instead, they should seek to do what is right and honorable in the eyes of everyone. This principle of non-retaliation aligns with restorative justice, which seeks to repair harm rather than perpetuate cycles of revenge.

Do not repay anyone evil for evil. (Romans 12:17)

2. Peace and Harmony: Paul emphasizes the importance of living at peace with everyone, as much as it depends on the individual. This pursuit of peace involves active efforts to reconcile and maintain harmonious relationships.

If it is possible, as far as it depends on you, live at peace with everyone. (Romans 12:18)

3. Leaving Vengeance to God: Paul counsels against taking personal revenge, urging believers to trust in God's justice. By leaving room for God's wrath, believers can focus on forgiveness and reconciliation, rather than seeking retribution.

Do not take revenge, my dear friends, but leave room for God's wrath. (Romans 12:19)

4. Active Kindness: Instead of responding to hostility with hostility, Paul encourages believers to respond with acts of kindness. Feeding a hungry enemy or giving drink to a thirsty foe not only addresses their immediate needs but also serves as a powerful gesture of reconciliation.

If your enemy is hungry, feed him; if he is thirsty, give him something to drink. (Romans 12:20)

5. Overcoming Evil with Good: Paul concludes with a call to overcome evil with good. This transformative approach seeks to break the cycle of evil by responding to wrongdoing with goodness and mercy, fostering healing and reconciliation.

Do not be overcome by evil, but overcome evil with good. (Romans 12:21)

2 Corinthians 5:18-21: The Ministry of Reconciliation

Context and Overview

In 2 Corinthians 5, Paul discusses the new creation that believers become through Christ. Verses 18-21 focus on the ministry of reconciliation, highlighting the role of believers as ambassadors for Christ, tasked with spreading the message of reconciliation.

All this is from God, who reconciled us to himself through Christ and gave us the ministry of reconciliation: that God was reconciling the world to himself in Christ, not counting people's sins against them. And he has committed to us the message of reconciliation. We are therefore Christ's ambassadors, as though God were making his appeal through us. We implore you on Christ's behalf: Be reconciled to God. God made him who had no sin to be sin for us, so that in him we might become the righteousness of God. (2 Corinthians 5:18-21)

Key Themes

1. Reconciliation with God: Paul begins by affirming that reconciliation originates from God, who reconciled humanity to Himself through Christ. This divine reconciliation serves as the foundation for all other acts of reconciliation.

All this is from God, who reconciled us to himself through Christ. (2 Corinthians 5:18)

2. The Ministry of Reconciliation: Believers are entrusted with the ministry of reconciliation, tasked with spreading the message that God is reconciling the world to Himself through Christ. This ministry emphasizes the importance of restoring broken relationships and promoting peace.

...and gave us the ministry of reconciliation. (2 Corinthians 5:18)

3. Ambassadors for Christ: Paul describes believers as ambassadors for Christ, representing Him and His message of reconciliation to the world. This ambassadorial role underscores the responsibility of believers to actively pursue and promote reconciliation.

We are therefore Christ's ambassadors, as though God were making his appeal through us. (2 Corinthians 5:20)

4. Not Counting Sins: Central to the message of reconciliation is the concept that God does not count people's sins against them. Instead, through Christ's sacrifice, believers are offered forgiveness and a restored relationship with God.

that God was reconciling the world to himself in Christ, not counting people's sins against them. (2 Corinthians 5:19)

5. Call to Be Reconciled: Paul implores his readers to be reconciled to God, emphasizing the urgency and importance of embracing this restored relationship.

We implore you on Christ's behalf: Be reconciled to God. (2 Corinthians 5:20)

6. Christ's Sacrifice: Paul concludes by highlighting the sacrificial act of Christ, who became sin for humanity so that believers might become the righteousness of God. This ultimate act of reconciliation sets the example for how believers should approach forgiveness and reconciliation in their own lives.

God made him who had no sin to be sin for us, so that in him we might become the righteousness of God. (2 Corinthians 5:21)

Practical Applications of Paul's Teachings

Forgiveness as a Cornerstone

Forgiveness is a central theme in Paul's teachings, and it is foundational to the practice of restorative justice. By forgiving others, believers can break the cycle of retaliation and promote healing.

1. Personal Forgiveness: Believers are called to forgive those who wrong them, reflecting the forgiveness they have received from God.

Bear with each other and forgive one another if any of you has a grievance against someone. Forgive as the Lord forgave you. (Colossians 3:13)

2. Community Forgiveness: Within the Christian community, forgiveness fosters unity and peace, allowing believers to live harmoniously.

Make every effort to keep the unity of the Spirit through the bond of peace. (Ephesians 4:3)

Pursuing Reconciliation

Reconciliation is not a passive process but an active pursuit. Paul's teachings encourage believers to take the initiative in restoring broken relationships.

1. Seeking Peace: Believers are urged to seek peace and reconciliation, taking proactive steps to resolve conflicts and restore harmony.

If it is possible, as far as it depends on you, live at peace with everyone. (Romans 12:18)

2. Restoring Relationships: Paul's instructions often include practical steps for restoring relationships, such as addressing grievances, offering forgiveness, and seeking mutual understanding.

Therefore, if you are offering your gift at the altar and there remember that your brother or sister has something against you, leave your gift there in front of the altar. First, go and be reconciled to them; then come and offer your gift. (Matthew 5:23-24)

Embodying the Ministry of Reconciliation

As ambassadors for Christ, believers are called to embody the ministry of reconciliation in their interactions with others.

1. Spreading the Message: Believers are tasked with spreading the message of reconciliation, encouraging others to embrace the forgiveness and restoration offered through Christ.

We are therefore Christ's ambassadors, as though God were making his appeal through us. (2 Corinthians 5:20)

2. Modeling Reconciliation: By modeling forgiveness and reconciliation in their own lives, believers can demonstrate the transformative power of these principles to others.

Be kind and compassionate to one another, forgiving each other, just as in Christ God forgave you. (Ephesians 4:32)

Paul's teachings on forgiveness and reconciliation provide a robust framework for understanding and practicing restorative justice within the Christian community. Through his letters, Paul emphasizes the importance of non-retaliation, active kindness, and the pursuit of peace. His teachings on the ministry of reconciliation highlight the divine origin of reconciliation and the responsibility of believers to spread this message and embody its principles.

By analyzing key passages such as Romans 12:17-21 and 2 Corinthians 5:18-21, we gain valuable insights into how forgiveness and reconciliation can transform individual lives and communities. As we continue to explore Paul's writings, we will see how these principles are further developed and applied, offering practical guidance for building a just, compassionate, and restorative society.

THE CONCEPT OF RECONCILIATION IN PAUL'S WRITINGS

Reconciliation is a central theme in the writings of Apostle Paul, encompassing both the vertical reconciliation between humanity and God and the horizontal reconciliation among individuals within the Christian community. Paul's epistles offer profound theological insights into the nature of reconciliation and practical guidance on how to live out this principle in daily life. This chapter explores Paul's concept of reconciliation, examining key passages that highlight its significance and implications.

Theological Foundations of Reconciliation

Reconciliation with God

At the heart of Paul's theology is the idea that humanity is reconciled to God through the sacrificial death and resurrection of Jesus Christ. This reconciliation is foundational to the Christian faith and serves as the basis for all other forms of reconciliation.

1. Restoration of Relationship: Paul teaches that through Christ, the broken relationship between humanity and God is restored. This restoration is not merely a cessation of hostility but a renewal of intimate fellowship with God.

All this is from God, who reconciled us to Himself through Christ and gave us the ministry of reconciliation. (2 Corinthians 5:18)

2. Justification and Forgiveness: Reconciliation involves justification and forgiveness, where believers are declared righteous before God and their sins are no longer counted against them.

that God was reconciling the world to himself in Christ, not counting people's sins against them. (2 Corinthians 5:19)

3. Peace with God: The result of reconciliation is peace with God, providing believers with a secure and harmonious relationship with their Creator.

Therefore, since we have been justified through faith, we have peace with God through our Lord Jesus Christ. (Romans 5:1)

Reconciliation Among Believers

Paul also emphasizes the importance of reconciliation within the Christian community, urging believers to restore broken relationships and live in harmony.

1. Unity in Christ: Paul teaches that all believers, regardless of their background, are united in Christ. This unity transcends cultural, social, and racial divisions, creating a new community of reconciled individuals.

There is neither Jew nor Gentile, neither slave nor free, nor is there male and female, for you are all one in Christ Jesus. (Galatians 3:28)

2. Ministry of Reconciliation: Believers are entrusted with the ministry of reconciliation, reflecting God's reconciliatory work by fostering peace and unity within the community.

We are therefore Christ's ambassadors, as though God were making his appeal through us. We implore you on Christ's behalf: Be reconciled to God. (2 Corinthians 5:20)

Key Passages on Reconciliation

2 Corinthians 5:18-21: The Ministry of Reconciliation

2 Corinthians 5:18-21 is a cornerstone passage that outlines Paul's theology of reconciliation and the role of believers in this divine mission.

All this is from God, who reconciled us to himself through Christ and gave us the ministry of reconciliation: that God was reconciling the world to himself in Christ, not counting people's sins against them. And he has committed to us the message of reconciliation. We are therefore Christ's ambassadors, as though God were making his appeal through us. We implore you on Christ's behalf: Be reconciled to God. God made him who had no sin to be sin for us, so that in him we might become the righteousness of God. (2 Corinthians 5:18-21)

1. Divine Initiative: Reconciliation begins with God, who takes the initiative to restore the broken relationship through Christ.

All this is from God, who reconciled us to Himself through Christ. (2 Corinthians 5:18)

2. Role of Believers: Believers are given the ministry of reconciliation, tasked with spreading the message that God is reconciling the world to Himself through Christ.

And he has committed to us the message of reconciliation. (2 Corinthians 5:19)

3. Ambassadors for Christ: As ambassadors, believers represent Christ and His message of reconciliation, urging others to be reconciled to God.

We are therefore Christ's ambassadors, as though God were making his appeal through us. (2 Corinthians 5:20)

4. Christ's Sacrifice: The basis of reconciliation is Christ's sacrificial death, where He took on sin so that believers might become the righteousness of God.

God made him who had no sin to be sin for us, so that in him we might become the righteousness of God. (2 Corinthians 5:21)

Romans 5:10-11: Reconciliation through Christ's Death

In Romans 5, Paul elaborates on the concept of reconciliation by highlighting the transformative power of Christ's death.

For if, while we were God's enemies, we were reconciled to him through the death of his Son, how much more, having been reconciled, shall we be saved through his life! Not only is this so, but we also boast in God through our Lord Jesus Christ, through whom we have now received reconciliation. (Romans 5:10-11)

1. From Enemies to Friends: Paul emphasizes the radical nature of reconciliation, where those who were once enemies of God are now reconciled through Christ's death.

For if, while we were God's enemies, we were reconciled to him through the death of his Son. (Romans 5:10)

2. Continuous Salvation: Reconciliation is not a one-time event but a continuous process of salvation through the life of Christ.

how much more, having been reconciled, shall we be saved through his life! (Romans 5:10)

3. Boasting in God: Believers can rejoice and boast in their restored relationship with God, celebrating the reconciliation received through Jesus Christ.

Not only is this so, but we also boast in God through our Lord Jesus Christ, through whom we have now received reconciliation. (Romans 5:11)

Ephesians 2:14-16: Breaking Down Dividing Walls

In Ephesians 2, Paul addresses the reconciliation between Jews and Gentiles, emphasizing how Christ's death has broken down the barriers that once separated them.

For he himself is our peace, who has made the two groups one and has destroyed the barrier, the dividing wall of hostility, by setting aside in his flesh the law with its commands and regulations. His purpose was to create in himself one new humanity out of the two, thus making peace, and in one body to reconcile both of them to God through the cross, by which he put to death their hostility. (Ephesians 2:14-16)

1. Christ as Peace: Christ is described as our peace, who unites previously divided groups into one body.

For he himself is our peace, who has made the two groups one. (Ephesians 2:14)

2. Destroying Hostility: Through His death, Christ destroys the barriers and hostility that separate people, creating a new, united humanity.

and has destroyed the barrier, the dividing wall of hostility. (Ephesians 2:14)

3. Reconciliation through the Cross: The cross is the means by which Christ reconciles both Jews and Gentiles to God, ending their hostility and creating peace.

in one body to reconcile both of them to God through the cross, by which he put to death their hostility. (Ephesians 2:16)

Practical Implications of Reconciliation

Living as Ambassadors of Reconciliation

Believers are called to live as ambassadors of reconciliation, actively promoting peace and restoring relationships within their communities.

1. Spreading the Message: As ambassadors, believers are tasked with sharing the message of reconciliation, encouraging others to be reconciled to God.

We are therefore Christ's ambassadors, as though God were making his appeal through us. (2 Corinthians 5:20)

2. Modeling Reconciliation: Believers should model reconciliation in their own lives, demonstrating forgiveness, compassion, and efforts to restore broken relationships.

Be kind and compassionate to one another, forgiving each other, just as in Christ God forgave you. (Ephesians 4:32)

Promoting Unity and Peace

Paul's teachings on reconciliation emphasize the importance of unity and peace within the Christian community.

1. Unity in Diversity: Believers are called to embrace unity in diversity, recognizing that they are all one in Christ regardless of their backgrounds.

There is neither Jew nor Gentile, neither slave nor free, nor is there male and female, for you are all one in Christ Jesus. (Galatians 3:28)

2. Pursuing Peace: Christians should actively pursue peace, seeking to resolve conflicts and build harmonious relationships within the community.

If it is possible, as far as it depends on you, live at peace with everyone. (Romans 12:18)

The Ministry of Reconciliation in Action

The Ministry of Reconciliation involves practical steps to restore relationships and promote peace.

1. Forgiveness and Repentance: Reconciliation often requires forgiveness and repentance, where both parties acknowledge their wrongs and seek to make amends.

Bear with each other and forgive one another if any of you has a grievance against someone. Forgive as the Lord forgave you. (Colossians 3:13)

2. Restorative Practices: Implementing restorative practices, such as mediation and reconciliation meetings, can help address conflicts and promote healing within the community.

If your brother or sister sins against you, go and point out their fault, just between the two of you. If they listen to you, you have won them over. (Matthew 18:15)

Reconciliation is a central theme in Paul's writings, reflecting both the theological foundation of reconciliation with God through Christ and the practical implications for reconciliation within the Christian community. Paul's teachings emphasize the transformative power of reconciliation, urging believers to embrace their role as ambassadors of Christ and actively promote peace and unity.

By exploring key passages such as 2 Corinthians 5:18-21, Romans 5:10-11, and Ephesians 2:14-16, we gain a deeper understanding of the significance of reconciliation in Paul's theology and its practical applications. As we continue to delve into Paul's letters, we will see how these principles are further developed and applied, offering valuable insights for building a just, compassionate, and restorative community.

FORGIVENESS AS A CORNERSTONE OF CHRISTIAN LIFE

Forgiveness is one of the fundamental principles of Christianity, emphasized throughout the teachings of Jesus and the writings of the Apostle Paul. It serves as a cornerstone for building and maintaining healthy, restorative relationships within the Christian community and with God. This chapter explores the concept of forgiveness in Paul's writings, its theological significance, and its practical application in the life of believers.

Theological Foundations of Forgiveness
Forgiveness as Divine Mandate

In Paul's theology, forgiveness is not merely a recommendation but a divine mandate grounded in the character and actions of God. Believers are called to forgive because they have been forgiven by God through Jesus Christ.

1. God's Forgiveness Through Christ: Paul emphasizes that forgiveness is a gift from God, made possible through the sacrificial death and resurrection of Jesus. This divine forgiveness is the model and foundation for human forgiveness.

In him we have redemption through his blood, the forgiveness of sins, in accordance with the riches of God's grace. (Ephesians 1:7)

2. Forgiveness as a Command: Paul instructs believers to forgive one another as an essential part of their faith, reflecting the forgiveness they have received from God.

Be kind and compassionate to one another, forgiving each other, just as in Christ God forgave you. (Ephesians 4:32)

Justification and Reconciliation

Forgiveness in Paul's writings is closely linked to the concepts of justification and reconciliation. It is through forgiveness that believers are justified before God and reconciled to Him.

1. Justification by Faith: Paul teaches that believers are justified, or declared righteous, by faith in Jesus Christ. This justification includes the forgiveness of sins, and removing the barrier between humanity and God.

Therefore, since we have been justified through faith, we have peace with God through our Lord Jesus Christ. (Romans 5:1)

2. Reconciliation with God: Forgiveness leads to reconciliation, restoring the broken relationship between humanity and God. This reconciliation is central to Paul's understanding of salvation.

All this is from God, who reconciled us to Himself through Christ and gave us the ministry of reconciliation. (2 Corinthians 5:18)

Key Passages on Forgiveness

Colossians 3:12-14: The Call to Forgive

In Colossians 3, Paul provides practical instructions for Christian living, emphasizing the importance of forgiveness within the community.

Therefore, as God's chosen people, holy and dearly loved, clothe yourselves with compassion, kindness, humility, gentleness, and patience. Bear with each other and forgive one another if any of you has a grievance against someone. Forgive as the Lord forgave you. And over these virtues put on love, which binds them all together in perfect unity. (Colossians 3:12-14)

1. Virtues of a Christian Life: Paul lists virtues that should characterize the lives of believers, including compassion, kindness, humility, gentleness, and patience. These virtues create a foundation for forgiveness.

Clothe yourselves with compassion, kindness, humility, gentleness and patience. (Colossians 3:12)

2. Bearing with One Another: Forgiveness involves bearing with each other's faults and extending grace, just as God has done for us.

Bear with each other and forgive one another if any of you has a grievance against someone. (Colossians 3:13)

3. Forgiving as the Lord Forgave: The standard for forgiveness is God's own forgiveness of believers. Paul urges Christians to forgive in the same way they have been forgiven by the Lord.

Forgive as the Lord forgave you. (Colossians 3:13)

4. Love and Unity: Forgiveness is tied to love, which binds all virtues together in perfect unity, promoting harmony and peace within the community.

And over these virtues put on love, which binds them all together in perfect unity. (Colossians 3:14)

Ephesians 4:31-32: Forgiveness and Compassion

In Ephesians 4, Paul contrasts behaviors that destroy community with those that build it up, highlighting forgiveness and compassion as essential elements of Christian conduct.

Get rid of all bitterness, rage and anger, brawling and slander, along with every form of malice. Be kind and compassionate to one another, forgiving each other, just as in Christ God forgave you. (Ephesians 4:31-32)

1. Removing Negative Behaviors: Paul calls believers to rid themselves of destructive behaviors such as bitterness, rage, anger, brawling, slander, and malice. These behaviors hinder forgiveness and reconciliation.

Get rid of all bitterness, rage and anger, brawling and slander, along with every form of malice. (Ephesians 4:31)

2. Kindness and Compassion: In place of these negative behaviors, believers are to exhibit kindness and compassion. These attitudes foster an environment where forgiveness can thrive.

Be kind and compassionate to one another. (Ephesians 4:32)

3. Forgiveness as a Reflection of Christ: Forgiveness is to be modeled after Christ's forgiveness, highlighting its divine origin and the need for believers to emulate this in their relationships.

Forgiving each other, just as in Christ God forgave you. (Ephesians 4:32)

Practical Applications of Forgiveness

Personal Forgiveness

Forgiveness begins at the personal level, where individuals choose to forgive those who have wronged them. This personal act of forgiveness is essential for healing and restoring relationships.

1. Choosing to Forgive: Forgiveness is a deliberate choice to release resentment and offer grace, even when it is difficult.

Bear with each other and forgive one another if any of you has a grievance against someone. Forgive as the Lord forgave you. (Colossians 3:13)

2. Healing and Freedom: Forgiveness brings healing to the wounded heart and freedom from the burden of bitterness and anger.

And forgive us our debts, as we also have forgiven our debtors. (Matthew 6:12)

Forgiveness Within the Community

Forgiveness within the Christian community is vital for maintaining unity and fostering a supportive and loving environment.

1. Promoting Unity: Forgiveness helps maintain unity within the community by resolving conflicts and preventing divisions.

Make every effort to keep the unity of the Spirit through the bond of peace. (Ephesians 4:3)

2. Modeling Christ's Love: By forgiving one another, believers model the love and grace of Christ, demonstrating the transformative power of the gospel.

Be kind and compassionate to one another, forgiving each other, just as in Christ God forgave you. (Ephesians 4:32)

Forgiveness in Action

Forgiveness is not just a theological concept but a practical action that believers must actively practice in their daily lives.

1. Seeking Reconciliation: Forgiveness often involves seeking reconciliation, where both parties come together to address the harm and restore the relationship.

Therefore, if you are offering your gift at the altar and there remember that your brother or sister has something against you, leave your gift there in front of the altar. First, go and be reconciled to them; then come and offer your gift. (Matthew 5:23-24)

2. Restorative Practices: Implementing restorative practices, such as mediation and reconciliation meetings, can help address conflicts and promote healing within the community.

If your brother or sister sins against you, go and point out their fault, just between the two of you. If they listen to you, you have won them over. (Matthew 18:15)

Challenges to Forgiveness

Overcoming Bitterness and Anger

Forgiveness can be challenging, especially when dealing with deep hurt and betrayal. Overcoming bitterness and anger is essential for true forgiveness.

1. Letting Go of Resentment: Paul urges believers to let go of bitterness, rage, and anger, which can hinder forgiveness and reconciliation.

Get rid of all bitterness, rage and anger, brawling and slander, along with every form of malice. (Ephesians 4:31)

2. Embracing Compassion: By embracing compassion and kindness, believers can create an environment where forgiveness becomes possible.

Be kind and compassionate to one another. (Ephesians 4:32)

The Process of Forgiveness

Forgiveness is often a process that takes time, involving multiple steps and a commitment to healing.

1. Acknowledging the Hurt: Recognizing and acknowledging the hurt is the first step toward forgiveness.

2. Choosing to Forgive: Making a deliberate decision to forgive, even if feelings of forgiveness are not immediately present.

3. Seeking God's Help: Relying on God's strength and grace to enable forgiveness, especially in difficult situations.

I can do all this through him who gives me strength. (Philippians 4:13)

Forgiveness is a cornerstone of the Christian life, deeply rooted in the teachings of Jesus and the writings of the Apostle Paul. It is essential for personal healing, maintaining unity within the community, and modeling the grace and love of God. Paul's writings provide profound theological insights and practical guidance on forgiveness, emphasizing its necessity and the transformative power it holds.

By exploring key passages such as Colossians 3:12-14 and Ephesians 4:31-32, we gain a deeper understanding of the importance of forgiveness and how to apply it in our daily lives. As we continue to study Paul's teachings, we are reminded of the central role forgiveness plays in building a just, compassionate, and restorative community, reflecting the heart of the gospel.

PRACTICAL APPLICATIONS OF FORGIVENESS IN THE CHURCH

Forgiveness is not only a theological concept but also a practical necessity within the Christian church. It is essential for maintaining healthy relationships, fostering community unity, and promoting spiritual growth. This chapter explores how forgiveness can be practically applied within the church, addressing common challenges and offering strategies for cultivating a forgiving and restorative community.

Building a Culture of Forgiveness

Teaching and Preaching on Forgiveness

1. Regular Sermons: Church leaders should regularly preach about forgiveness, highlighting its biblical foundations and practical implications. This consistent teaching can help embed forgiveness into the fabric of the church's culture.

Forgive as the Lord forgave you. (Colossians 3:13)

2. Bible Studies and Workshops: Organizing Bible studies and workshops focused on forgiveness can provide deeper insights and practical tools for congregation members to practice forgiveness in their daily lives.

Be kind and compassionate to one another, forgiving each other, just as in Christ God forgave you. (Ephesians 4:32)

Modeling Forgiveness

1. Leadership Example: Church leaders must model forgiveness in their interactions. By demonstrating forgiveness and reconciliation in their own lives, leaders set a powerful example for the congregation to follow.

Follow my example, as I follow the example of Christ. (1 Corinthians 11:1)

2. Personal Testimonies: Sharing personal testimonies of forgiveness can inspire others and provide tangible examples of how forgiveness can transform relationships and lives.

They triumphed over him by the blood of the Lamb and by the word of their testimony. (Revelation 12:11)

Practical Steps to Facilitate Forgiveness

Encouraging Open Communication

1. Conflict Resolution Mechanisms: Establish clear conflict resolution mechanisms within the church to address grievances and facilitate open communication. This can include mediation teams, counseling services, and designated conflict resolution meetings.

If your brother or sister sins against you, go and point out their fault, just between the two of you. If they listen to you, you have won them over. (Matthew 18:15)

2. Safe Spaces for Dialogue: Create safe spaces where individuals can express their feelings and work through conflicts without fear of judgment or retaliation. This can be achieved through small groups, support groups, and confidential counseling sessions.

Speak the truth in love, and we will grow to become in every respect the mature body of him who is the head, that is, Christ. (Ephesians 4:15)

Promoting Reconciliation Practices

1. Mediation and Counseling: Provide mediation and counseling services to help individuals and groups navigate conflicts and work towards reconciliation. Skilled mediators can facilitate discussions that lead to understanding and forgiveness.

If it is possible, as far as it depends on you, live at peace with everyone. (Romans 12:18)

2. Restorative Justice Circles: Implement restorative justice circles where all parties involved in a conflict can come together to discuss the harm caused, share their perspectives, and agree on steps to make amends.

Therefore, if you are offering your gift at the altar and there remember that your brother or sister has something against you, leave your gift there in front of the altar. First go and be reconciled to them; then come and offer your gift. (Matthew 5:23-24)

Forgiveness in Church Discipline

1. Restorative Discipline: When church discipline is necessary, it should be carried out with the goal of restoration rather than punishment. The process should include opportunities for the offender to repent, make amends, and be reintegrated into the community.

Brothers and sisters, if someone is caught in a sin, you who live by the Spirit should restore that person gently. But watch yourselves, or you also may be tempted. (Galatians 6:1)

2. Supporting Both Parties: Provide support for both the offender and the victim during the discipline process. This can include counseling, accountability partners, and prayer support.

Bear one another's burdens, and so fulfill the law of Christ. (Galatians 6:2)

Addressing Common Challenges to Forgiveness

Overcoming Resistance to Forgiveness

1. Teaching on the Benefits of Forgiveness: Educate the congregation on the spiritual, emotional, and relational

benefits of forgiveness. Understanding the positive impacts can motivate individuals to embrace forgiveness.

Forgive, and you will be forgiven. Give, and it will be given to you. (Luke 6:37-38)

2. Providing Practical Tools: Offer practical tools and resources, such as books, workshops, and counseling, to help individuals work through their resistance to forgiveness.

I can do all this through him who gives me strength. (Philippians 4:13)

Dealing with Deep Hurt and Betrayal

1. Acknowledging the Pain: Encourage individuals to acknowledge their pain and hurt as a first step towards healing. Validating their feelings can help them move towards forgiveness.

The Lord is close to the brokenhearted and saves those who are crushed in spirit. (Psalm 34:18)

2. Seeking God's Healing: Guide individuals to seek God's healing through prayer, scripture, and the support of the church community.

He heals the brokenhearted and binds up their wounds. (Psalm 147:3)

Forgiveness in Action

Encouraging Acts of Reconciliation

1. Acts of Kindness: Encourage individuals to perform acts of kindness towards those who have wronged them. These acts can break down barriers and foster a spirit of reconciliation.

If your enemy is hungry, feed him; if he is thirsty, give him something to drink. (Romans 12:20)

2. Public Reconciliation: When appropriate, public acts of reconciliation, such as apologies and forgiveness during church services, can demonstrate the power of forgiveness and set an example for the congregation.

Confess your sins to each other and pray for each other so that you may be healed. (James 5:16)

Long-Term Support and Accountability

1. Ongoing Support Groups: Establish support groups for individuals who are struggling with forgiveness. These groups can provide a safe space for sharing experiences, receiving encouragement, and holding each other accountable.

Let us consider how we may spur one another on toward love and good deeds. (Hebrews 10:24)

2. Accountability Partners: Pair individuals with accountability partners who can walk with them through the process of forgiveness and reconciliation, offering prayer, support, and encouragement.

Two are better than one because they have a good return for their labor: If either of them falls down, one can help the other up. (Ecclesiastes 4:9-10)

Forgiveness is a vital aspect of Christian life and community, essential for maintaining healthy relationships and promoting spiritual growth. By building a culture of forgiveness through teaching, modeling, and practical steps, the church can become a place of healing and restoration.

Addressing common challenges to forgiveness and providing ongoing support and accountability are crucial for helping individuals embrace forgiveness and live it out in their daily lives. As the church embodies the principles of forgiveness and reconciliation, it reflects the heart of the gospel and becomes a powerful witness to the transformative power of God's grace.

Through the practical applications of forgiveness outlined in this chapter, the church can foster an environment where forgiveness thrives, relationships are restored, and the love of Christ is tangibly demonstrated. By continually seeking to forgive as the Lord has forgiven us, the church can build a community characterized by peace, unity, and compassion.

CHAPTER 05

COMMUNITY AND ACCOUNTABILITY IN PAUL'S EPISTLES

Apostle Paul's epistles provide a wealth of guidance on the role of the church as a restorative community, emphasizing the importance of mutual accountability, support, and reconciliation. Paul envisioned the church as a body of believers working together to nurture spiritual growth, restore broken relationships, and maintain communal harmony. This chapter explores how Paul's teachings can help the church function as a restorative community, fostering accountability and support among its members.

The Church as the Body of Christ

Unity and Diversity in the Body

Paul frequently uses the metaphor of the church as the body of Christ to illustrate the interconnectedness and interdependence of believers.

1. Unity in Diversity: Paul teaches that the church, like a human body, is made up of diverse members with different functions, yet it is united in Christ.

Just as a body, though one, has many parts, but all its many parts form one body, so it is with Christ. (1 Corinthians 12:12)

2. Interdependence: Each member of the body is essential and contributes to the overall health and function of the church. This interdependence emphasizes the need for mutual support and accountability.

If one part suffers, every part suffers with it; if one part is honored, every part rejoices with it. (1 Corinthians 12:26)

Building Up the Body

Paul emphasizes the importance of building up the church, encouraging believers to use their gifts for the common good and to support one another in love.

1. Edification: Believers are called to use their spiritual gifts to edify the church, promoting spiritual growth and strengthening the community.

To each one the manifestation of the Spirit is given for the common good. (1 Corinthians 12:7)

2. Love as the Foundation: Paul underscores that love is the foundation for all interactions within the church, guiding how believers should treat one another.

And now these three remain faith, hope, and love. But the greatest of these is love. (1 Corinthians 13:13)

Mutual Accountability

Bearing One Another's Burdens

Paul teaches that believers should bear one another's burdens, providing support and accountability to help each other overcome challenges and grow in faith.

1. Shared Responsibility: Bearing one another's burdens reflects the shared responsibility of the church community to support and uplift each other.

Carry each other's burdens, and in this way you will fulfill the law of Christ. (Galatians 6:2)

2. Restoring Gently: When addressing sin within the community, Paul advises believers to restore one another gently, highlighting the restorative approach to accountability.

Brothers and sisters, if someone is caught in a sin, you who live by the Spirit should restore that person gently. But watch yourselves, or you also may be tempted. (Galatians 6:1)

Accountability and Encouragement

Paul encourages the church to hold each other accountable while also providing encouragement and support to foster spiritual growth and perseverance.

1. Exhortation: Believers are called to exhort one another, offering constructive feedback and encouragement to spur each other on toward love and good deeds.

And let us consider how we may spur one another on toward love and good deeds. (Hebrews 10:24)

2. Encouragement: Encouraging one another is vital for building up the community and helping individuals remain steadfast in their faith.

Therefore encourage one another and build each other up, just as in fact you are doing. (1 Thessalonians 5:11)

Reconciliation and Restoration

The Ministry of Reconciliation

Paul's concept of the ministry of reconciliation emphasizes the church's role in restoring broken relationships and fostering peace within the community.

1. Divine Reconciliation: Believers are called to reconcile with God and each other, reflecting the reconciliation achieved through Christ.

All this is from God, who reconciled us to Himself through Christ and gave us the ministry of reconciliation. (2 Corinthians 5:18)

2. Ambassadors of Reconciliation: As ambassadors of Christ, believers are tasked with spreading the message of reconciliation and embodying its principles in their interactions.

We are therefore Christ's ambassadors, as though God were making his appeal through us. We implore you on Christ's behalf: Be reconciled to God. (2 Corinthians 5:20)

Practical Steps for Reconciliation

Paul provides practical guidance for resolving conflicts and restoring relationships within the church.

1. Addressing Offenses: Believers are encouraged to address offenses directly and seek reconciliation, fostering a spirit of forgiveness and unity.

If your brother or sister sins against you, go and point out their fault, just between the two of you. If they listen to you, you have won them over. (Matthew 18:15)

2. Forgiveness and Restoration: Forgiveness is a crucial step in the reconciliation process, allowing individuals to move past grievances and restore fellowship.

Bear with each other and forgive one another if any of you has a grievance against someone. Forgive as the Lord forgave you. (Colossians 3:13)

Fostering a Supportive Community

Encouraging One Another

Paul frequently emphasizes the importance of mutual encouragement to strengthen the community and promote spiritual growth.

1. Speaking Life: Believers are called to speak words of encouragement and life to one another, building each other up in faith.

Do not let any unwholesome talk come out of your mouths, but only what is helpful for building others up according to their needs, that it may benefit those who listen. (Ephesians 4:29)

2. Supporting the Weak: Providing support for those who are weak or struggling is a vital aspect of a supportive community.

We who are strong ought to bear with the failings of the weak and not to please ourselves. (Romans 15:1)

Cultivating a Culture of Care

A restorative community is marked by genuine care and concern for one another, reflecting the love of Christ.

1. Loving One Another: Love is the defining characteristic of a Christian community, and believers are called to love one another deeply.

Above all, love each other deeply, because love covers over a multitude of sins. (1 Peter 4:8)

2. Acts of Service: Serving one another in practical ways demonstrates care and builds a strong, supportive community.

Serve one another humbly in love. (Galatians 5:13)

Challenges to Building a Restorative Community

Overcoming Division and Strife

Paul addresses the challenges of division and strife within the church, urging believers to seek unity and reconciliation.

1. Addressing Factions: Paul calls for the elimination of factions and divisions, promoting unity and harmony within the community.

I appeal to you, brothers and sisters, in the name of our Lord Jesus Christ, that all of you agree with one another in what you say and that there be no divisions among you, but that you be perfectly united in mind and thought. (1 Corinthians 1:10)

2. Pursuing Peace: Believers are encouraged to pursue peace actively and resolve conflicts in a Christlike manner.

Make every effort to live in peace with everyone and to be holy; without holiness, no one will see the Lord. (Hebrews 12:14)

Addressing Sin and Accountability

Addressing sin within the community is a necessary but challenging aspect of building a restorative church.

1. Gentle Correction: Paul advises that correction should be done gently and with the goal of restoration, rather than punishment.

Brothers and sisters, if someone is caught in a sin, you who live by the Spirit should restore that person gently. (Galatians 6:1)

2. Community Support: Providing support and accountability for those struggling with sin helps them overcome their challenges and grow in their faith.

Encourage the disheartened, help the weak, be patient with everyone. (1 Thessalonians 5:14)

Paul's vision of the church as a restorative community is rooted in the principles of mutual accountability, support, and reconciliation. By viewing the church as the body of Christ, Paul emphasizes the interconnectedness and interdependence of believers, highlighting the importance of building each other up in love and maintaining unity.

Through practical steps such as bearing one another's burdens, fostering a culture of care, and addressing conflicts with a restorative approach, the church can embody the principles of a restorative community. By following Paul's teachings, believers can create a church environment where forgiveness, reconciliation, and support thrive, reflecting the heart of the gospel and the love of Christ.

As we continue to explore Paul's epistles, we will gain further insights into how to apply these principles in our own church communities, fostering a just, compassionate, and restorative environment that nurtures spiritual growth and promotes communal harmony.

MUTUAL ACCOUNTABILITY AND SUPPORT AMONG BELIEVERS

Mutual accountability and support are fundamental aspects of the Christian faith, as emphasized by Apostle Paul in his epistles. Paul envisioned the church as a community where believers encourage, correct, and support one another in their spiritual journeys. This chapter explores the principles of mutual accountability and support among believers, highlighting key passages from Paul's writings and their practical applications in fostering a healthy, restorative church community.

The Biblical Basis for Mutual Accountability

The Body of Christ

Paul uses the metaphor of the church as the body of Christ to illustrate the interconnectedness and mutual responsibility of believers.

1. Interdependence: Just as the parts of the human body are interdependent, so are the members of the church. Each member plays a vital role in the health and function of the body.

Just as a body, though one, has many parts, but all its many parts form one body, so it is with Christ. (1 Corinthians 12:12)

2. Mutual Care: The members of the body must care for one another, recognizing that the well-being of each individual affects the whole community.

If one part suffers, every part suffers with it; if one part is honored, every part rejoices with it. (1 Corinthians 12:26)

The Law of Christ

Paul teaches that believers fulfill the law of Christ by bearing one another's burdens, highlighting the importance of mutual support and accountability.

1. Bearing Burdens: Helping each other with burdens and challenges is a practical way to live out the law of Christ, which is rooted in love.

Carry each other's burdens, and in this way you will fulfill the law of Christ. (Galatians 6:2)

2. Restoring Gently: When addressing sin within the community, Paul advises believers to restore one another gently, reflecting a restorative approach to accountability.

Brothers and sisters, if someone is caught in a sin, you who live by the Spirit should restore that person gently. But watch yourselves, or you also may be tempted. (Galatians 6:1)

Practical Steps for Mutual Accountability

Encouraging One Another

Encouragement is a key aspect of mutual accountability, helping believers stay strong in their faith and committed to their spiritual growth.

1. Daily Encouragement: Paul urges believers to encourage one another daily to prevent the hardening of hearts by sin's deceitfulness.

But encourage one another daily, as long as it is called "Today," so that none of you may be hardened by sin's deceitfulness. (Hebrews 3:13)

2. Building Each Other Up: Words of encouragement and affirmation build up the community, fostering a supportive environment.

Therefore encourage one another and build each other up, just as in fact you are doing. (1 Thessalonians 5:11)

Speaking the Truth in Love

Honest communication, rooted in love, is essential for maintaining accountability within the church.

1. Truthful Communication: Speaking the truth in love helps believers grow in maturity and unity, promoting a healthy community.

Instead, of speaking the truth in love, we will grow to become in every respect the mature body of him who is the head, that is, Christ. (Ephesians 4:15)

2. Addressing Issues: When issues arise, addressing them truthfully and lovingly helps prevent misunderstandings and fosters reconciliation.

If your brother or sister sins against you, go and point out their fault, just between the two of you. If they listen to you, you have won them over. (Matthew 18:15)

Providing Support and Care

Mutual support involves practical acts of care and assistance, helping each other through life's challenges.

1. Practical Assistance: Providing practical help to those in need reflects the love and care of the community.

Share with the Lord's people who are in need. Practice hospitality. (Romans 12:13)

2. Emotional and Spiritual Support: Offering emotional and spiritual support through prayer, counseling,

and companionship strengthens the bonds within the community.

Rejoice with those who rejoice; mourn with those who mourn. (Romans 12:15)

Accountability in Practice

Confession and Forgiveness

Confession and forgiveness are integral to maintaining mutual accountability and restoring relationships within the church.

1. Confessing Sins: Confessing sins to one another fosters transparency and accountability, allowing for mutual support in overcoming struggles.

Therefore confess your sins to each other and pray for each other so that you may be healed. (James 5:16)

2. Extending Forgiveness: Forgiveness restores broken relationships and promotes unity within the community.

Bear with each other and forgive one another if any of you has a grievance against someone. Forgive as the Lord forgave you. (Colossians 3:13)

Encouraging Spiritual Growth

Accountability involves encouraging each other in spiritual disciplines and growth, and helping believers stay committed to their faith.

1. Accountability Partners: Establishing accountability partnerships can provide ongoing support and encouragement for personal spiritual disciplines such as prayer, Bible study, and service.

Two are better than one because they have a good return for their labor: If either of them falls down, one can help the other up. (Ecclesiastes 4:9-10)

2. Mentoring Relationships: Older and more mature believers can mentor younger believers, providing guidance, wisdom, and support in their spiritual journeys.

Likewise, teach the older women to be reverent in the way they live... Then they can urge the younger women to love their husbands and children. (Titus 2:3-4)

Handling Conflict

Addressing and resolving conflicts is crucial for maintaining mutual accountability and peace within the church.

1. Biblical Process for Conflict Resolution: Paul outlines a process for addressing conflicts, emphasizing direct communication and reconciliation.

If your brother or sister sins, go and point out their fault, just between the two of you. If they listen to you, you have won them over. But if they will not listen, take one or two others along, so that 'every matter may be established by the testimony of two or three witnesses.' If they still refuse to listen, tell it to the church. (Matthew 18:15-17)

2. Peacemaking: Believers are called to be peacemakers, actively seeking to resolve conflicts and promote harmony.

Blessed are the peacemakers, for they will be called children of God. (Matthew 5:9)

Building a Culture of Mutual Accountability

Teaching and Preaching on Accountability

Regular teaching and preaching on the importance of mutual accountability can help embed this principle into the church's culture.

1. Biblical Teaching: Emphasizing the biblical basis for mutual accountability in sermons and Bible studies can reinforce its importance.

All Scripture is God-breathed and is useful for teaching, rebuking, correcting, and training in righteousness. (2 Timothy 3:16)

2. Practical Application: Providing practical examples and applications of accountability can help congregation members understand how to live it out in their daily lives.

Do not merely listen to the word, and so deceive yourselves. Do what it says. (James 1:22)

Creating Structures for Accountability

Establishing structures and systems within the church can facilitate mutual accountability and support.

1. Small Groups: Small groups provide a setting for deeper relationships, where members can hold each other accountable and offer support.

Every day they continued to meet together in the temple courts. They broke bread in their homes and ate together with glad and sincere hearts. (Acts 2:46)

2. Accountability Teams: Forming accountability teams or support groups can provide structured opportunities for members to share their struggles and successes and receive encouragement.

And let us consider how we may spur one another on toward love and good deeds. (Hebrews 10:24)

Mutual accountability and support are essential components of a healthy, restorative church community. By fostering an environment where believers encourage, correct, and support one another, the church can help its members grow in their faith and maintain spiritual vitality. Paul's teachings provide a robust framework for understanding and practicing mutual accountability, emphasizing the importance of love, truth, and practical support.

By implementing practical steps such as encouraging one another, speaking the truth in love, providing support, and handling conflicts biblically, the church can build a culture of mutual accountability that reflects the heart of the gospel. As we continue to explore Paul's epistles, we gain further insights into how to apply these principles in our own church communities, fostering a just, compassionate, and restorative environment that nurtures spiritual growth and promotes communal harmony.

ADDRESSING SIN AND CONFLICT WITHIN THE COMMUNITY

Addressing sin and conflict within the Christian community is a crucial aspect of maintaining a healthy, restorative church environment. Apostle Paul's teachings provide practical guidance on how believers can confront sin and resolve conflicts in a manner that promotes healing, restoration, and unity. This chapter explores Paul's instructions on dealing with sin and conflict, emphasizing the principles outlined in passages like Galatians 6:1-2.

Principles of Addressing Sin and Conflict

Gentle Restoration

Paul's approach to addressing sin within the community is marked by a spirit of gentleness and a focus on restoration rather than punishment.

1. Gentle Correction: In Galatians 6:1, Paul advises believers to restore those caught in sin gently. This gentle approach ensures that the goal is to bring about repentance and healing rather than condemnation.

Brothers and sisters, if someone is caught in a sin, you who live by the Spirit should restore that person gently. But watch yourselves, or you also may be tempted. (Galatians 6:1)

2. Self-Reflection: Paul warns those correcting others to be mindful of their own vulnerabilities, promoting humility and self-awareness in the process.

But watch yourselves, or you also may be tempted. (Galatians 6:1)

Bearing One Another's Burdens

Paul emphasizes the importance of mutual support and accountability in dealing with sin and conflict, encouraging believers to bear one another's burdens.

1. Shared Responsibility: Bearing each other's burdens reflects the collective responsibility of the church to support one another through difficulties, including dealing with sin.

Carry each other's burdens, and in this way you will fulfill the law of Christ. (Galatians 6:2)

2. Fulfilling the Law of Christ: By bearing one another's burdens, believers fulfill the law of Christ, which is centered on love and compassion.

Carry each other's burdens, and in this way you will fulfill the law of Christ. (Galatians 6:2)

Practical Steps for Addressing Sin and Conflict

Direct Communication

Addressing sin and conflict directly and privately is the first step in resolving issues within the community.

1. One-on-One Dialogue: Jesus instructs believers to address issues directly with the person involved, promoting private and respectful communication.

If your brother or sister sins, go and point out their fault, just between the two of you. If they listen to you, you have won them over. (Matthew 18:15)

2. Seeking Understanding: Engaging in open dialogue helps to clarify misunderstandings and fosters mutual understanding, which is essential for resolution.

The purposes of a person's heart are deep waters, but one who has insight draws them out. (Proverbs 20:5)

Involving Others When Necessary

If direct communication does not resolve the conflict, involving a few others can help mediate and facilitate resolution.

1. Mediation: Bringing one or two others into the discussion can provide additional perspectives and help mediate the conflict.

But if they will not listen, take one or two others along, so that 'every matter may be established by the testimony of two or three witnesses.' (Matthew 18:16)

2. Seeking Counsel: Involving wise and respected members of the community can provide valuable counsel and support in resolving the conflict.

Plans fail for lack of counsel, but with many advisers, they succeed. (Proverbs 15:22)

Bringing the Issue to the Church

If the conflict remains unresolved, bringing the issue before the broader church community ensures transparency and collective support.

1. Community Involvement: Involving the church helps to ensure that the resolution process is fair and inclusive, promoting communal accountability.

If they still refuse to listen, tell it to the church. (Matthew 18:17)

2. Collective Wisdom: The collective wisdom of the church can provide a balanced and just resolution to the conflict.

For lack of guidance a nation falls, but victory is won through many advisers. (Proverbs 11:14)

The Role of Forgiveness and Reconciliation

Emphasizing Forgiveness

Forgiveness is a crucial component in resolving conflict and addressing sin, promoting healing and restoring relationships.

1. Command to Forgive: Paul instructs believers to forgive one another, mirroring the forgiveness they have received from God.

Bear with each other and forgive one another if any of you has a grievance against someone. Forgive as the Lord forgave you. (Colossians 3:13)

2. Healing Power of Forgiveness: Forgiveness facilitates emotional and spiritual healing, allowing both parties to move forward in unity.

Be kind and compassionate to one another, forgiving each other, just as in Christ God forgave you. (Ephesians 4:32)

Seeking Reconciliation

Reconciliation goes beyond forgiveness, involving the restoration of relationships and the rebuilding of trust.

1. Pursuit of Peace: Believers are called to actively pursue peace and reconciliation, seeking to mend broken relationships.

If it is possible, as far as it depends on you, live at peace with everyone. (Romans 12:18)

2. Restorative Practices: Implementing restorative practices, such as mediation and reconciliation circles, helps to address the harm and facilitate healing.

Therefore, if you are offering your gift at the altar and there remember that your brother or sister has something against you, leave your gift there in front of the altar. First, go and be reconciled to them; then come and offer your gift. (Matthew 5:23-24)

Building a Culture of Accountability

Teaching and Preaching

Regular teaching and preaching on the importance of accountability and the process for addressing sin and conflict can help embed these principles into the church's culture.

1. Biblical Instruction: Providing biblical instruction on handling sin and conflict ensures that the church is grounded in scriptural principles.

All Scripture is God-breathed and is useful for teaching, rebuking, correcting, and training in righteousness. (2 Timothy 3:16)

2. Practical Application: Offering practical applications and examples helps believers understand how to apply these principles in their daily lives.

Do not merely listen to the word, and so deceive yourselves. Do what it says. (James 1:22)

Creating Safe Spaces for Dialogue

Creating safe spaces where individuals can express their concerns and address conflicts without fear of judgment is essential for fostering accountability.

1. Confidential Counseling: Providing confidential counseling services can help individuals address their issues privately and receive guidance.

Plans fail for lack of counsel, but with many advisers, they succeed. (Proverbs 15:22)

2. Support Groups: Establishing support groups for various struggles can offer a community of understanding and accountability.

Let us not give up meeting together, as some are in the habit of doing, but encouraging one another—and all the more as you see the Day approaching. (Hebrews 10:25)

Addressing sin and conflict within the community is a crucial aspect of maintaining a healthy, restorative church environment. Paul's teachings provide a comprehensive framework for handling these issues with gentleness, humility, and a focus on restoration. By following the principles outlined in passages like Galatians 6:1-2, believers can create a culture of mutual accountability and support that promotes healing and unity.

Through direct communication, involving others when necessary, and bringing unresolved issues before the church, conflicts can be addressed in a manner that honors God and strengthens the community. Emphasizing forgiveness and reconciliation ensures that relationships are not only restored but also deepened, reflecting the transformative power of the gospel.

By embedding these principles into the church's culture through teaching, preaching, and creating safe spaces for dialogue, the church can become a beacon of love, grace, and restorative justice. As we continue to explore Paul's epistles, we gain further insights into how to apply these principles in our own church communities, fostering a just, compassionate, and restorative environment that nurtures spiritual growth and promotes communal harmony.

RESTORATIVE PRACTICES IN CHURCH DISCIPLINE

Church discipline is a challenging yet essential aspect of maintaining the health and integrity of a Christian community. Apostle Paul provides valuable guidance on how to handle church discipline in a manner that is restorative rather than punitive. In passages like 1 Corinthians 5, Paul addresses the need for discipline within the church while emphasizing the ultimate goal of restoration and reconciliation. This chapter explores Paul's teachings on church discipline and offers practical insights into implementing restorative practices within the church.

Biblical Foundation for Church Discipline

Purpose of Church Discipline

The primary purposes of church discipline, according to Paul, are to maintain the purity of the church, restore the sinner, and protect the community from harmful behavior.

1. Purity of the Church: Paul emphasizes the importance of maintaining the moral and spiritual purity of the church, which reflects Christ's holiness.

Get rid of the old yeast, so that you may be a new unleavened batch—as you really are. For Christ, our Passover lamb, has been sacrificed. (1 Corinthians 5:7)

2. Restoration of the Sinner: The goal of discipline is not merely to punish but to lead the sinner to repentance and restoration within the community.

So that his spirit may be saved on the day of the Lord. (1 Corinthians 5:5)

3. Protection of the Community: Discipline also serves to protect the church community from behaviors that can cause division, harm, and spiritual decay.

Don't you know that a little yeast leavens the whole batch of dough? (1 Corinthians 5:6)

Principles of Restorative Discipline

Paul's approach to church discipline is characterized by principles that aim to restore rather than simply exclude.

1. Confrontation with Love: Addressing sin within the church should be done with a spirit of love and concern for the individual's well-being.

If your brother or sister sins, go and point out their fault, just between the two of you. If they listen to you, you have won them over. (Matthew 18:15)

2. Opportunity for Repentance: The disciplinary process should provide the individual with opportunities to repent and seek reconciliation.

Godly sorrow brings repentance that leads to salvation and leaves no regret, but worldly sorrow brings death. (2 Corinthians 7:10)

3. Reintegration into the Community: The ultimate aim of discipline is to restore the individual to full fellowship within the church once repentance and reconciliation have occurred.

Now instead, you ought to forgive and comfort him, so that he will not be overwhelmed by excessive sorrow. I urge you, therefore, to reaffirm your love for him. (2 Corinthians 2:7-8)

Case Study: 1 Corinthians 5

The Situation in Corinth

In 1 Corinthians 5, Paul addresses a specific case of immorality within the Corinthian church, where a man was involved in an incestuous relationship with his stepmother. The church had failed to address this issue, and Paul provides instructions on how to handle the situation.

1. Public Sin: The sin in question was well-known and publicly scandalous, necessitating a response from the church.

It is actually reported that there is sexual immorality among you, and of a kind that even pagans do not tolerate: A man is sleeping with his father's wife. (1 Corinthians 5:1)

2. Lack of Action: The church's failure to address the sin indicated a lack of discernment and concern for the community's purity.

And you are proud! Shouldn't you rather have gone into mourning and have put out of your fellowship the man who has been doing this? (1 Corinthians 5:2)

Paul's Instructions for Discipline

Paul provides clear instructions on how to handle the situation, emphasizing the need for both firm action and a restorative approach.

1. Expulsion from Fellowship: Paul instructs the church to remove the individual from their fellowship to protect the community and prompt the sinner to repentance.

Hand this man over to Satan for the destruction of the flesh, so that his spirit may be saved on the day of the Lord. (1 Corinthians 5:5)

2. Restorative Intent: The purpose of this action is not to condemn but to bring about repentance and ultimately save the individual's spirit.

Hand this man over to Satan for the destruction of the flesh, so that his spirit may be saved on the day of the Lord. (1 Corinthians 5:5)

3. Purity of the Community: Removing the sinner helps to preserve the moral and spiritual integrity of the church.

Get rid of the old yeast, so that you may be a new unleavened batch—as you really are. For Christ, our Passover lamb, has been sacrificed. (1 Corinthians 5:7)

Implementing Restorative Practices

Steps for Restorative Church Discipline

Implementing restorative practices in church discipline involves a structured process that aims to balance justice with mercy, and firmness with compassion.

1. Initial Confrontation: Address the sin privately with the individual, offering them the opportunity to acknowledge their wrongdoing and seek repentance.

If your brother or sister sins, go and point out their fault, just between the two of you. If they listen to you, you have won them over. (Matthew 18:15)

2. Involving Mediators: If the individual does not respond to private confrontation, involve one or two others to help mediate and encourage repentance.

But if they will not listen, take one or two others along, so that 'every matter may be established by the testimony of two or three witnesses.' (Matthew 18:16)

3. Church Involvement: If the individual still refuses to repent, bring the matter before the church community to seek a collective resolution.

If they still refuse to listen, tell it to the church. (Matthew 18:17)

4. Temporary Separation: As a last resort, if the individual remains unrepentant, consider a temporary separation from the church fellowship to emphasize the seriousness of the sin and encourage repentance.

Hand this man over to Satan for the destruction of the flesh, so that his spirit may be saved on the day of the Lord. (1 Corinthians 5:5)

5. Path to Restoration: Throughout the process, maintain a clear path for restoration, outlining the steps the individual can take to be reconciled with the church and reinstated into the fellowship.

Now instead, you ought to forgive and comfort him, so that he will not be overwhelmed by excessive sorrow. I urge you, therefore, to reaffirm your love for him. (2 Corinthians 2:7-8)

Supporting Both the Offender and the Community

A restorative approach to church discipline involves supporting both the offender and the community throughout the process.

1. Counseling and Support: Provide counseling and support for the individual involved in the sin, helping them understand the impact of their actions and guiding them towards repentance.

Carry each other's burdens, and in this way you will fulfill the law of Christ. (Galatians 6:2)

2. Community Healing: Offer support to the community affected by the sin, addressing their concerns and fostering a spirit of forgiveness and reconciliation.

Encourage one another and build each other up, just as in fact you are doing. (1 Thessalonians 5:11)

3. Prayer and Intercession: Engage the church in prayer and intercession for the individual and the community, seeking God's guidance and grace throughout the disciplinary process.

And pray in the Spirit on all occasions with all kinds of prayers and requests. With this in mind, be alert and always keep on praying for all the Lord's people. (Ephesians 6:18)

Challenges and Considerations

Balancing Justice and Mercy

One of the key challenges in restorative church discipline is balancing justice and mercy, ensuring that the process is both fair and compassionate.

1. Firmness and Compassion: Discipline should be firm enough to address the seriousness of sin but compassionate enough to offer hope and a path to restoration.

Let your gentleness be evident to all. The Lord is near. (Philippians 4:5)

2. Consistency and Flexibility: While maintaining consistency in the application of discipline, it is also important to consider individual circumstances and be flexible in finding the best approach for each situation.

But the wisdom that comes from heaven is first of all pure; then peace-loving, considerate, submissive, full of mercy and good fruit, impartial and sincere. (James 3:17)

Maintaining Confidentiality

Confidentiality is crucial in handling church discipline to protect the dignity and privacy of the individuals involved.

1. Discretion: Ensure that discussions about disciplinary matters are conducted with discretion, involving only those necessary for the process.

A gossip betrays confidence, but a trustworthy person keeps a secret. (Proverbs 11:13)

2. Protecting Reputations: Avoid public shaming or unnecessary disclosure of details, focusing on the goal of restoration and healing.

Above all, love each other deeply, because love covers over a multitude of sins. (1 Peter 4:8)

Restorative practices in church discipline, as outlined by Apostle Paul, emphasize the need for a balanced approach that addresses sin while promoting repentance and reconciliation

By following the principles of gentle correction, bearing one another's burdens, and providing a clear path to restoration, the church can handle disciplinary matters in a way that honors God and strengthens the community.

Implementing these restorative practices requires careful planning, sensitivity, and a commitment to the spiritual well-being of both the individual and the church. By supporting both the offender and the community, maintaining confidentiality, and balancing justice with mercy, the church can create an environment where discipline leads to growth, healing, and deeper fellowship.

As we continue to explore Paul's teachings, we gain further insights into how to apply these principles in our own church communities, fostering a just, compassionate, and restorative environment that nurtures spiritual growth and promotes communal harmony.

CHAPTER 06

PAUL'S APPROACH TO JUSTICE AND MERCY

Apostle Paul's teachings offer a profound balance between justice and mercy, reflecting the heart of the gospel message. In his epistles, Paul emphasizes the necessity of upholding justice while simultaneously extending mercy and grace. This balance is crucial for fostering a restorative Christian community that honors God's righteousness and compassion. This chapter explores how Paul navigates the tension between justice and mercy in his writings, providing practical insights for applying these principles within the church.

Theological Foundations of Justice and Mercy

Justice in Paul's Teachings

Paul's understanding of justice is deeply rooted in the character of God, who is both just and righteous. Justice, according to Paul, involves upholding God's standards of holiness and fairness.

1. God's Righteousness: Paul emphasizes that God's justice is an expression of His righteousness, requiring that sin be addressed and dealt with appropriately.

For in the gospel the righteousness of God is revealed—a righteousness that is by faith from first to last, just as it is written: "The righteous will live by faith." (Romans 1:17)

2. Impartiality: Paul teaches that God's justice is impartial, treating all people equally and without favoritism.

For God does not show favoritism. (Romans 2:11)

3. Judgment: Justice involves the right judgment of sin, which Paul acknowledges as necessary to uphold God's holiness.

For we must all appear before the judgment seat of Christ, so that each of us may receive what is due us for the things done while in the body, whether good or bad. (2 Corinthians 5:10)

Mercy in Paul's Teachings

Paul equally emphasizes the importance of mercy, which is central to the gospel message. Mercy involves showing compassion and forgiveness to those who have wronged us, reflecting God's gracious character.

1. God's Mercy: Paul often speaks of God's mercy as the foundation of salvation, highlighting that it is by God's mercy that believers are saved.

But because of his great love for us, God, who is rich in mercy, made us alive with Christ even when we were dead in transgressions—it is by grace you have been saved. (Ephesians 2:4-5)

2. Forgiveness: Mercy is expressed through forgiveness, which Paul encourages believers to practice as they have been forgiven by God.

Bear with each other and forgive one another if any of you has a grievance against someone. Forgive as the Lord forgave you. (Colossians 3:13)

3. Compassion: Paul calls believers to be compassionate, showing kindness and mercy to others as an expression of their faith.

Be kind and compassionate to one another, forgiving each other, just as in Christ God forgave you. (Ephesians 4:32)

Balancing Justice and Mercy in Paul's Writings

Addressing Sin with Justice and Mercy

Paul's approach to addressing sin within the community reflects a balance between justice and mercy, ensuring that sin is dealt with appropriately while providing opportunities for repentance and restoration.

1. Confronting Sin: Paul does not shy away from confronting sin, recognizing the need for justice in maintaining the purity and integrity of the church.

It is actually reported that there is sexual immorality among you, and of a kind that even pagans do not tolerate: A man is sleeping with his father's wife. (1 Corinthians 5:1)

2. Offering Restoration: Even as Paul calls for discipline, he also emphasizes the importance of restoring the sinner to fellowship upon repentance.

Now instead, you ought to forgive and comfort him, so that he will not be overwhelmed by excessive sorrow. I urge you, therefore, to reaffirm your love for him. (2 Corinthians 2:7-8)

The Example of the Corinthian Church

The situation in the Corinthian church, as addressed in 1 Corinthians 5 and 2 Corinthians 2, provides a clear example of how Paul balances justice and mercy.

1. Initial Discipline: Paul instructs the Corinthian church to expel the immoral man from their fellowship to uphold justice and purity.

Hand this man over to Satan for the destruction of the flesh, so that his spirit may be saved on the day of the Lord. (1 Corinthians 5:5)

2. Call for Mercy: Upon the man's repentance, Paul urges the church to forgive and comfort him, demonstrating mercy and facilitating his restoration.

Now instead, you ought to forgive and comfort him, so that he will not be overwhelmed by excessive sorrow. I urge you, therefore, to reaffirm your love for him. (2 Corinthians 2:7-8)

Practical Applications for the Church

Implementing Just and Merciful Practices

Paul's teachings provide a framework for implementing practices within the church that balance justice and mercy.

1. Establishing Clear Guidelines: Churches should establish clear guidelines for addressing sin and conflict, ensuring that justice is upheld while allowing for mercy and restoration.

But everything should be done in a fitting and orderly way. (1 Corinthians 14:40)

2. Creating a Path for Restoration: Discipline processes should include a clear path for the offender to repent and be restored to full fellowship.

If we confess our sins, he is faithful and just and will forgive us our sins and purify us from all unrighteousness. (1 John 1:9)

3. Supporting Both the Offender and the Community: Providing support for both the offender and the community ensures that justice and mercy are experienced by all parties involved.

Encourage one another and build each other up, just as in fact you are doing. (1 Thessalonians 5:11)

Encouraging a Culture of Compassion

Creating a culture of compassion within the church helps to balance justice with mercy, fostering an environment where forgiveness and restoration are prioritized.

1. Teaching on Mercy: Regular teaching and preaching on the importance of mercy and forgiveness helps to cultivate a compassionate community.

Blessed are the merciful, for they will be shown mercy. (Matthew 5:7)

2. Modeling Compassion: Church leaders should model compassion and forgiveness in their interactions, setting an example for the congregation.

Be kind and compassionate to one another, forgiving each other, just as in Christ God forgave you. (Ephesians 4:32)

3. Practicing Forgiveness: Encouraging members to practice forgiveness in their daily lives helps to embed mercy into the church's culture.

Bear with each other and forgive one another if any of you has a grievance against someone. Forgive as the Lord forgave you. (Colossians 3:13)

Challenges in Balancing Justice and Mercy

Overcoming Legalism

Legalism can hinder the practice of mercy, emphasizing strict adherence to rules at the expense of compassion and forgiveness.

1. Avoiding Harshness: Churches must guard against harsh, legalistic approaches that lack mercy and fail to reflect the grace of the gospel.

Woe to you, teachers of the law and Pharisees, you hypocrites! You give a tenth of your spices—mint, dill, and cumin. But you have neglected the more important matters of the law—justice, mercy, and faithfulness. You should have practiced the latter, without neglecting the former. (Matthew 23:23)

2. Emphasizing Grace: Emphasizing the grace and mercy of God helps to counteract legalistic tendencies and promote a balanced approach to discipline.

For it is by grace you have been saved, through faith—and this is not from yourselves, it is the gift of God. (Ephesians 2:8)

Addressing Recidivism

Dealing with repeat offenders poses a challenge in balancing justice and mercy, as there is a need to protect the community while offering opportunities for repentance.

1. Clear Consequences: Establishing clear consequences for repeated offenses helps to uphold justice while maintaining the possibility of restoration.

If they still refuse to listen, tell it to the church; and if they refuse to listen even to the church, treat them as you would a pagan or a tax collector. (Matthew 18:17)

2. Ongoing Support: Providing ongoing support and accountability for repeat offenders helps them to overcome their struggles and encourages genuine repentance.

Carry each other's burdens, and in this way you will fulfill the law of Christ. (Galatians 6:2)

Balancing justice and mercy is a vital aspect of Paul's teachings, reflecting the heart of the gospel and the character of God. Paul's approach to church discipline, as seen in his epistles, emphasizes the need for justice in addressing sin while also extending mercy and facilitating restoration. By following Paul's principles, churches can create a culture that upholds righteousness and fosters compassion.

Implementing just and merciful practices, encouraging a culture of compassion, and addressing challenges such as legalism and recidivism are essential for maintaining this balance. As the church navigates the tension between justice and mercy, it can provide a powerful witness to the transformative power of the gospel, promoting healing, unity, and spiritual growth within the community.

As we continue to explore Paul's epistles, we gain further insights into how to apply these principles in our own church communities, fostering a just, compassionate, and restorative environment that nurtures spiritual growth and promotes communal harmony.

THE SIGNIFICANCE OF GRACE AND REDEMPTION UNDERSTANDING

Grace and redemption are central themes in the teachings of Apostle Paul, forming the foundation of his understanding of the Christian faith. Paul's epistles emphasize that salvation is a gift from God, rooted in His grace, and made possible through the redemptive work of Jesus Christ. This chapter explores the significance of grace and redemption in Paul's writings, highlighting their transformative power and practical implications for believers.

Understanding Grace

Definition and Nature of Grace

Grace, in Paul's theology, is the unmerited favor and kindness of God extended to humanity. It is not earned or deserved but freely given by God out of His love and mercy.

1. Unmerited Favor: Grace is a gift from God that cannot be earned by human efforts. It is given freely to those who believe in Jesus Christ.

For it is by grace you have been saved, through faith—and this is not from yourselves, it is the gift of God—not by works, so that no one can boast. (Ephesians 2:8-9)

2. Divine Initiative: Grace originates from God's initiative, demonstrating His love and mercy towards humanity.

But because of his great love for us, God, who is rich in mercy, made us alive with Christ even when we were dead in transgressions—it is by grace you have been saved. (Ephesians 2:4-5)

The Role of Grace in Salvation

Grace is foundational to the process of salvation. It is through grace that believers are justified, sanctified, and ultimately glorified.

1. Justification by Grace: Believers are justified—declared righteous—by God's grace through faith in Jesus Christ.

He saved us, not because of righteous things we had done, but because of his mercy. He saved us through the washing of rebirth and renewal by the Holy Spirit. (Titus 3:5)

2. Sanctification through Grace: Grace also plays a crucial role in sanctification, the process of being made holy and growing in Christlikeness.

For the grace of God has appeared that offers salvation to all people. It teaches us to say "No" to ungodliness and worldly passions and to live self-controlled, upright, and godly lives in this present age. (Titus 2:11-12)

3. Glorification by Grace: Ultimately, grace leads to the glorification of believers, where they are fully transformed and brought into God's eternal presence.

And those he predestined, he also called; those he called, he also justified; those he justified, he also glorified. (Romans 8:30)

The Concept of Redemption

Redemption through Christ

Redemption, in Paul's writings, refers to the act of being delivered from sin and its consequences through the sacrificial death and resurrection of Jesus Christ.

1. Ransom for Sin: Christ's death on the cross serves as a ransom, paying the price for humanity's sin and securing their freedom.

In him we have redemption through his blood, the forgiveness of sins, in accordance with the riches of God's grace. (Ephesians 1:7)

2. Deliverance from Sin's Power: Redemption not only forgives sin but also delivers believers from its power, enabling them to live in newness of life.

For we know that our old self was crucified with him so that the body ruled by sin might be done away with, that we should no longer be slaves to sin. (Romans 6:6)

The Scope of Redemption

Redemption in Paul's theology has both a personal and cosmic dimension, impacting individuals and the entire creation.

1. Personal Redemption: Individually, redemption brings believers into a restored relationship with God, transforming their lives and destinies.

Therefore, if anyone is in Christ, the new creation has come: The old has gone, the new is here! (2 Corinthians 5:17)

2. Cosmic Redemption: Paul also speaks of cosmic redemption, where all of creation will be liberated from its

bondage to decay and brought into the freedom and glory of the children of God.

For the creation waits in eager expectation for the children of God to be revealed. (Romans 8:19)

Practical Implications of Grace and Redemption

Living in the Light of Grace

Paul encourages believers to live lives that reflect the grace they have received, characterized by gratitude, humility, and holiness.

1. Gratitude: Recognizing that salvation is a gift of grace should lead believers to live with deep gratitude towards God.

Give thanks in all circumstances; for this is God's will for you in Christ Jesus. (1 Thessalonians 5:18)

2. Humility: Grace eliminates boasting, fostering humility among believers as they acknowledge their dependence on God's mercy.

For it is by grace you have been saved, through faith—and this is not from yourselves, it is the gift of God—not by works, so that no one can boast. (Ephesians 2:8-9)

3. Holiness: Grace empowers believers to live holy lives, rejecting sin and pursuing righteousness.

For the grace of God has appeared that offers salvation to all people. It teaches us to say "No" to ungodliness and worldly passions, and to live self-controlled, upright and godly lives in this present age. (Titus 2:11-12)

Embracing the Reality of Redemption

Living in the reality of redemption involves embracing the new identity and freedom found in Christ.

1. New Identity: Believers are called to embrace their new identity in Christ, living as children of God and heirs of His promises.

So in Christ Jesus you are all children of God through faith. (Galatians 3:26)

2. Freedom from Sin: Redemption delivers believers from the power of sin, enabling them to live in the freedom and victory of Christ.

It is for freedom that Christ has set us free. Stand firm, then, and do not let yourselves be burdened again by a yoke of slavery. (Galatians 5:1)

3. Hope for the Future: Redemption provides believers with a future hope, anticipating the full realization of God's promises and the renewal of all things.

We wait eagerly for our adoption to sonship, the redemption of our bodies. (Romans 8:23)

Transformative Power of Grace and Redemption

Personal Transformation

Grace and redemption bring about profound personal transformation, changing the believer's relationship with God and others.

1. Restored Relationship with God: Through grace and redemption, believers are reconciled to God, experiencing His love and presence in their lives.

Therefore, since we have been justified through faith, we have peace with God through our Lord Jesus Christ. (Romans 5:1)

2. Changed Relationships with Others: Grace and redemption also transform relationships with others, promoting forgiveness, reconciliation, and love.

Be kind and compassionate to one another, forgiving each other, just as in Christ God forgave you. (Ephesians 4:32)

Communal Transformation

The principles of grace and redemption extend to the entire community, fostering a culture of grace, forgiveness, and mutual support.

1. Grace-Filled Community: Churches are called to be grace-filled communities, reflecting the grace they have received in their interactions with one another.

Bear with each other and forgive one another if any of you has a grievance against someone. Forgive as the Lord forgave you. (Colossians 3:13)

2. Supportive Fellowship: Redemption leads to a supportive fellowship where believers bear each other's burdens and encourage one another in their faith.

Carry each other's burdens, and in this way you will fulfill the law of Christ. (Galatians 6:2)

Grace and redemption are central to Paul's understanding of the Christian faith, highlighting the unmerited favor of God and the transformative power of Christ's sacrificial work. These themes underscore the nature of salvation as a gift and the profound impact it has on the lives of believers.

By embracing the reality of grace and redemption, believers can live lives characterized by gratitude, humility, holiness, and freedom. These principles not only transform individuals but also shape the entire community, fostering a culture of grace, forgiveness, and mutual support.

As we continue to explore Paul's epistles, we gain deeper insights into how to apply the principles of grace and redemption in our own lives and communities, nurturing a restorative and transformative environment that reflects the heart of the gospel.

CASE STUDIES FROM PAUL'S LETTERS

Apostle Paul's letters provide practical examples of how the principles of grace, redemption, justice, and mercy are applied in real-life situations within the early Christian communities. Through specific case studies, such as those found in Philemon and 1 Corinthians 6:1-8, Paul demonstrates how these theological principles can be lived out in the context of community relationships and conflicts. This chapter explores these case studies, offering insights into how Paul's teachings can guide contemporary church practices.

The Case of Philemon: Grace and Redemption in Action

Background of the Letter to Philemon

The letter to Philemon is one of Paul's shortest epistles, yet it powerfully illustrates the principles of grace and redemption. Paul writes to Philemon, a Christian leader, on behalf of Onesimus, a runaway slave who has become a believer.

1. Onesimus' Transformation: Onesimus, once a slave and possibly a thief, has been transformed by his encounter with Paul and his newfound faith in Christ.

I am sending him—who is my very heart—back to you. (Philemon 1:12)

2. Paul's Appeal: Paul appeals to Philemon to receive Onesimus not as a slave but as a beloved brother in Christ, emphasizing the radical equality and transformation brought about by the gospel.

Perhaps the reason he was separated from you for a little while was that you might have him back forever— no longer as a slave, but better than a slave, as a dear brother. (Philemon 1:15-16)

Application of Grace and Redemption

Paul's letter to Philemon highlights several key principles of grace and redemption.

1. Transformation through Redemption: Onesimus' new identity in Christ transforms his relationship with Philemon. Paul underscores that in Christ, social barriers and past wrongs are transcended.

So if you consider me a partner, welcome him as you would welcome me. (Philemon 1:17)

2. Appeal for Forgiveness: Paul urges Philemon to forgive Onesimus and to show him the same grace that he himself has received from God.

If he has done you any wrong or owes you anything, charge it to me. I, Paul, am writing this with my own hand. I will pay it back—not to mention that you owe me your very self. (Philemon 1:18-19)

3. Restorative Justice: Rather than demanding justice through punishment, Paul advocates for a restorative approach that seeks reconciliation and restoration of relationships.

I do wish, brother, that I may have some benefit from you in the Lord; refresh my heart in Christ. (Philemon 1:20)

The Case of 1 Corinthians 6:1-8: Resolving Disputes within the Church

Background of the Passage

In 1 Corinthians 6:1-8, Paul addresses the issue of Christians taking legal disputes against each other to secular courts. He challenges the Corinthian believers to handle their disputes within the church community.

1. Internal Disputes: Paul is concerned that the public litigation of disputes among believers damages the church's witness and undermines its unity.

If any of you has a dispute with another, do you dare to take it before the ungodly for judgment instead of before the Lord's people? (1 Corinthians 6:1)

2. Call to Internal Resolution: Paul emphasizes the competence of the church to judge such matters, highlighting the community's ability to mediate and resolve conflicts.

Or do you not know that the Lord's people will judge the world? And if you are to judge the world, are you not competent to judge trivial cases? (1 Corinthians 6:2)

Application of Justice and Mercy

Paul's instructions in 1 Corinthians 6:1-8 offer valuable lessons on applying justice and mercy in resolving disputes within the church.

1. Avoiding Public Scandal: Paul warns against airing grievances before unbelievers, which can bring the church into disrepute. Instead, he advocates for resolving conflicts within the Christian community.

But instead, one brother takes another to court—and this in front of unbelievers! (1 Corinthians 6:6)

2. Community Accountability: The church is called to act as a community of accountability, where disputes can be addressed and resolved with wisdom and fairness.

Therefore, if you have disputes about such matters, do you ask for a ruling from those whose way of life is scorned in the church? (1 Corinthians 6:4)

3. Emphasis on Reconciliation: Paul emphasizes the importance of reconciliation over legal victory, urging believers to seek peace and unity.

The very fact that you have lawsuits among you means you have been completely defeated already. Why not rather be wronged? Why not rather be cheated? (1 Corinthians 6:7)

Practical Lessons from Paul's Case Studies

Promoting Forgiveness and Reconciliation

Both case studies from Philemon and 1 Corinthians highlight the importance of forgiveness and reconciliation within the Christian community.

1. Forgiveness as a Response to Grace: Just as Philemon is urged to forgive Onesimus, believers are called to forgive others in light of the grace they have received from God.

Bear with each other and forgive one another if any of you has a grievance against someone. Forgive as the Lord forgave you. (Colossians 3:13)

2. Reconciliation as a Priority: Paul's exhortation to the Corinthians to resolve disputes internally underscores the priority of reconciliation over legalistic justice.

Blessed are the peacemakers, for they will be called children of God. (Matthew 5:9)

Upholding Justice with Mercy

Paul's approach balances the need for justice with the imperative of mercy, aiming for outcomes that restore relationships and uphold community integrity.

1. Restorative Justice: In both cases, Paul seeks restorative justice that heals relationships rather than punitive justice that merely enforces rules.

Now instead, you ought to forgive and comfort him, so that he will not be overwhelmed by excessive sorrow. (2 Corinthians 2:7)

2. Community Mediation: Encouraging the church to handle disputes internally promotes a culture of mutual accountability and support, ensuring that justice is administered with mercy.

If your brother or sister sins, go and point out their fault, just between the two of you. If they listen to you, you have won them over. (Matthew 18:15)

Empowering the Community

Paul's teachings empower the Christian community to take an active role in maintaining justice and mercy within their fellowship.

1. Competence of the Church: Paul affirms the church's ability to judge and resolve conflicts, encouraging believers to trust in their community's wisdom and guidance.

Or do you not know that the Lord's people will judge the world? (1 Corinthians 6:2)

2. Active Participation: By involving the community in the process of discipline and reconciliation, Paul promotes active participation and shared responsibility among believers.

Carry each other's burdens, and in this way you will fulfill the law of Christ. (Galatians 6:2)

The case studies from Paul's letters to Philemon and the Corinthians provide practical insights into applying the principles of grace, redemption, justice, and mercy within the Christian community. Through these examples, Paul demonstrates how to navigate complex relational dynamics with a focus on restoration and reconciliation.

By promoting forgiveness and reconciliation, upholding justice with mercy, and empowering the community to take an active role in conflict resolution, Paul's teachings offer a timeless framework for fostering a healthy and restorative church environment. As contemporary believers, we can draw on these principles to address our own conflicts and challenges, creating communities that reflect the transformative power of the gospel.

As we continue to study Paul's epistles, we gain deeper understanding and practical guidance for living out these principles in our own lives and church communities, nurturing a culture of grace, justice, and mercy that honors God and strengthens our fellowship.

IMPLEMENTING JUSTICE AND MERCY IN A CONTEMPORARY SETTING

The principles of justice and mercy, as taught by Apostle Paul, are timeless and relevant for the church today. Implementing these principles in contemporary settings requires thoughtful application and a commitment to fostering a restorative community. This chapter explores practical ways to incorporate justice and mercy within modern church contexts, addressing common challenges and providing strategies for effective ministry.

Understanding the Balance of Justice and Mercy

Defining Justice and Mercy

To effectively implement justice and mercy, it is essential to understand their definitions and how they complement each other.

1. Justice: In the biblical context, justice involves upholding what is right, fair, and equitable. It includes addressing wrongdoing, maintaining order, and protecting the vulnerable.

For I, the Lord, love justice; I hate robbery and wrongdoing. In my faithfulness, I will reward my people and make an everlasting covenant with them. (Isaiah 61:8)

2. Mercy: Mercy is the compassionate treatment of those in distress, offering forgiveness and kindness even when it is undeserved. It reflects God's grace and love toward humanity.

Be merciful, just as your Father is merciful. (Luke 6:36)

Integrating Justice and Mercy

Paul's teachings emphasize the need to integrate justice and mercy, ensuring that discipline and correction are tempered with compassion and forgiveness.

1. Restorative Justice: This approach focuses on repairing harm and restoring relationships rather than merely punishing wrongdoing.

Brothers and sisters, if someone is caught in a sin, you who live by the Spirit should restore that person gently. (Galatians 6:1)

2. Merciful Accountability: Holding individuals accountable for their actions while offering pathways for repentance and reconciliation embodies the balance of justice and mercy.

Bear with each other and forgive one another if any of you has a grievance against someone. Forgive as the Lord forgave you. (Colossians 3:13)

Implementing Justice in the Church

Establishing Fair and Transparent Processes

To uphold justice, churches need to establish fair and transparent processes for addressing issues and conflicts.

1. Clear Guidelines: Develop clear guidelines and procedures for handling disciplinary matters, ensuring that they are consistent and just.

But everything should be done in a fitting and orderly way. (1 Corinthians 14:40)

2. Due Process: Ensure that all parties involved in a dispute or disciplinary action receive fair treatment and the opportunity to present their perspectives.

The first to speak in court sounds right—until the cross-examination begins. (Proverbs 18:17)

Protecting the Vulnerable

Justice involves actively protecting and advocating for the vulnerable within the church community.

1. Safeguarding Policies: Implement safeguarding policies to protect children, the elderly, and other vulnerable members from harm and abuse.

Defend the weak and the fatherless; uphold the cause of the poor and the oppressed. (Psalm 82:3)

2. Support Systems: Create support systems for individuals who have experienced harm or injustice, providing counseling, advocacy, and practical assistance.

Religion that God our Father accepts as pure and faultless is this: to look after orphans and widows in their distress and to keep oneself from being polluted by the world. (James 1:27)

Implementing Mercy in the Church

Cultivating a Culture of Forgiveness

Mercy is expressed through forgiveness, which should be a foundational value within the church.

1. Teaching Forgiveness: Regularly teach and preach on the importance of forgiveness, using biblical examples and practical applications.

Forgive as the Lord forgave you. (Colossians 3:13)

2. Modeling Forgiveness: Church leaders should model forgiveness in their own lives, demonstrating how to forgive others and seek reconciliation.

Be kind and compassionate to one another, forgiving each other, just as in Christ God forgave you. (Ephesians 4:32)

Providing Compassionate Care

Mercy also involves providing compassionate care to those in need, reflecting the love and grace of Christ.

1. Benevolence Ministries: Establish benevolence ministries that offer practical assistance, such as food, clothing, and financial support, to those in need.

If anyone has material possessions and sees a brother or sister in need but has no pity on them, how can the love of God be in that person? (1 John 3:17)

2. Pastoral Care: Develop pastoral care programs that provide emotional and spiritual support to individuals facing difficult circumstances.

Carry each other's burdens, and in this way you will fulfill the law of Christ. (Galatians 6:2)

Integrating Justice and Mercy in Conflict Resolution

Mediation and Reconciliation Processes

Effective conflict resolution requires integrating justice and mercy through mediation and reconciliation processes.

1. Mediation Teams: Form mediation teams within the church to help facilitate the resolution of conflicts and promote reconciliation.

If your brother or sister sins, go and point out their fault, just between the two of you. If they listen to you, you have won them over. (Matthew 18:15)

2. Reconciliation Programs: Develop reconciliation programs that provide structured opportunities for parties in conflict to address issues, seek forgiveness, and restore relationships.

Blessed are the peacemakers, for they will be called children of God. (Matthew 5:9)

Restorative Discipline

Discipline should aim to restore rather than merely punish, reflecting both justice and mercy.

1. Restorative Practices: Use restorative practices that focus on repairing harm and rebuilding trust, such as restorative circles and accountability partnerships.

Now instead, you ought to forgive and comfort him, so that he will not be overwhelmed by excessive sorrow. (2 Corinthians 2:7)

2. Pathways to Restoration: Provide clear pathways for individuals to be restored to full fellowship after discipline, including opportunities for repentance, restitution, and reconciliation.

If we confess our sins, he is faithful and just and will forgive us our sins and purify us from all unrighteousness. (1 John 1:9)

Addressing Challenges in Implementing Justice and Mercy

Overcoming Resistance to Change

Implementing justice and mercy may encounter resistance, especially when it involves changing long-standing practices or addressing deeply ingrained attitudes.

1. Education and Training: Provide education and training for church leaders and members on the biblical foundations and practical applications of justice and mercy.

All Scripture is God-breathed and is useful for teaching, rebuking, correcting, and training in righteousness. (2 Timothy 3:16)

2. Change Management: Use change management strategies to facilitate the transition to new practices, including clear communication, involvement of key stakeholders, and gradual implementation.

Be completely humble and gentle; be patient, bearing with one another in love. (Ephesians 4:2)

Maintaining Balance

Maintaining a balance between justice and mercy requires ongoing attention and intentionality.

1. Regular Review: Regularly review disciplinary and conflict resolution processes to ensure they are fair, just, and merciful.

The way of the righteous is like the first gleam of dawn, which shines ever brighter until the full light of day. (Proverbs 4:18)

2. Feedback Mechanisms: Establish feedback mechanisms that allow members to provide input and share their experiences, helping to identify areas for improvement.

Plans fail for lack of counsel, but with many advisers, they succeed. (Proverbs 15:22)

Implementing justice and mercy in contemporary church settings is essential for creating a restorative community that reflects the heart of the gospel. By understanding and integrating these principles, churches can address conflicts, protect the vulnerable, and promote reconciliation and healing.

Through fair and transparent processes, compassionate care, and restorative practices, churches can uphold justice while extending mercy. Overcoming resistance and maintaining balance requires ongoing education, review, and feedback, ensuring that the church remains a place of grace and truth.

As we continue to study Paul's epistles and apply their teachings, we can build communities that embody justice and mercy, fostering environments where individuals are valued, relationships are restored, and God's love is made manifest.

CHAPTER 07

RESTORATIVE JUSTICE IN PAUL'S LETTER TO PHILEMON

The letter to Philemon is a unique and personal epistle in the New Testament, showcasing Apostle Paul's approach to restorative justice within the early Christian community. This brief but powerful letter addresses the issue of a runaway slave, Onesimus, and his relationship with his master, Philemon. Through this letter, Paul demonstrates the principles of grace, forgiveness, and reconciliation, offering a profound example of restorative justice in action. This chapter delves into the background and context of the letter to Philemon, exploring its themes and significance.

Background and Context of the Letter

Historical and Cultural Setting

The letter to Philemon was written by Apostle Paul during his imprisonment, likely in Rome, around AD 60-62.

It is one of the so-called "Prison Epistles," along with Ephesians, Philippians, and Colossians.

1. Philemon: Philemon was a wealthy Christian and a leader in the church at Colossae. He was known for his love and faith towards Jesus and his hospitality towards fellow believers.

I always thank my God as I remember you in my prayers because I hear about your love for all his holy people and your faith in the Lord Jesus. (Philemon 1:4-5)

2. Onesimus: Onesimus was a slave belonging to Philemon who had run away, possibly stealing from his master in the process. He eventually met Paul and became a Christian.

Formerly he was useless to you, but now he has become useful both to you and to me. (Philemon 1:11)

3. Roman Slavery: Understanding the context of Roman slavery is crucial. Slavery was a pervasive institution in the Roman Empire, with slaves often being treated as property. However, the early Christian teachings began to challenge these norms, promoting the inherent value and equality of all individuals.

Purpose and Themes

Paul's letter to Philemon serves multiple purposes, addressing personal, relational, and theological issues.

1. Appeal for Onesimus: The primary purpose of the letter is to appeal to Philemon to receive Onesimus back not as a slave, but as a beloved brother in Christ.

Perhaps the reason he was separated from you for a little while was that you might have him back forever— no longer as a slave, but better than a slave, as a dear brother. (Philemon 1:15-16)

2. Restorative Justice: The letter embodies the principles of restorative justice, focusing on reconciliation and the restoration of relationships rather than punishment.

So if you consider me a partner, welcome him as you would welcome me. (Philemon 1:17)

3. Transformation through the Gospel: Paul emphasizes the transformative power of the gospel, which changes social dynamics and personal relationships, reflecting the new identity in Christ.

For we were all baptized by one Spirit so as to form one body—whether Jews or Gentiles, slave or free—and we were all given the one Spirit to drink. (1 Corinthians 12:13)

Analysis of Key Passages

Paul's Appeal for Onesimus

Paul's approach in appealing for Onesimus is marked by tact, respect, and a deep understanding of Christian love and fellowship.

1. A Personal Plea: Paul begins with a personal appeal to Philemon, acknowledging their relationship and Philemon's character.

Therefore, although in Christ I could be bold and order you to do what you ought to do, yet I prefer to appeal to you on the basis of love. It is as none other than Paul—an old man and now also a prisoner of Christ Jesus— that I appeal to you for my son Onesimus. (Philemon 1:8-10)

2. Transformation of Onesimus: Paul highlights the transformation that has occurred in Onesimus' life, indicating that he is no longer just a slave but a valuable and beloved brother in Christ.

Formerly he was useless to you, but now he has become useful both to you and to me. (Philemon 1:11)

3. Voluntary Return: Paul points out that Onesimus is returning voluntarily, demonstrating his repentance and willingness to reconcile.

I am sending him—who is my very heart—back to you. (Philemon 1:12)

The Call for Reconciliation

Paul's call for reconciliation between Philemon and Onesimus is rooted in the Christian principles of forgiveness and unity in Christ.

1. Equal Standing in Christ: Paul emphasizes the equal standing of Onesimus in Christ, urging Philemon to see him as a brother rather than a slave.

So if you consider me a partner, welcome him as you would welcome me. (Philemon 1:17)

2. Forgiveness and Restoration: Paul encourages Philemon to forgive any wrongs and to restore Onesimus to his household, not as a servant but as a fellow believer.

If he has done you any wrong or owes you anything, charge it to me. (Philemon 1:18)

3. Partnership in Faith: By asking Philemon to welcome Onesimus as he would welcome Paul, Paul is calling for a radical change in their relationship, based on their common faith and partnership in the gospel.

Confident of your obedience, I write to you, knowing that you will do even more than I ask. (Philemon 1:21)

Theological Implications

The Power of the Gospel

The letter to Philemon highlights the transformative power of the gospel, which breaks down social barriers and creates a new community of equals in Christ.

1. New Identity in Christ: Onesimus' new identity as a Christian transcends his former status as a slave, reflecting the inclusive nature of the Christian community.

Here there is no Gentile or Jew, circumcised or uncircumcised, barbarian, Scythian, slave or free, but Christ is all and is in all. (Colossians 3:11)

2. Unity and Equality: Paul's appeal for Onesimus underscores the unity and equality that believers share in Christ, challenging existing social hierarchies and norms.

There is neither Jew nor Gentile, neither slave nor free, nor is there male and female, for you are all one in Christ Jesus. (Galatians 3:28)

Restorative Justice and Christian Ethics

Paul's approach in the letter exemplifies the principles of restorative justice, focusing on healing and reconciliation rather than retribution.

1. Restoration over Retribution: By advocating for Onesimus' restoration rather than punishment, Paul models a form of justice that seeks to repair relationships and promote peace.

If you forgive anyone, I also forgive him. And what I have forgiven—if there was anything to forgive—I have forgiven in the sight of Christ for your sake, in order that

Satan might not outwit us. For we are not unaware of his schemes. (2 Corinthians 2:10-11)

2. Ethical Living: The letter also highlights the ethical implications of the gospel, calling believers to live out their faith through acts of mercy, forgiveness, and reconciliation.

Be kind and compassionate to one another, forgiving each other, just as in Christ God forgave you. (Ephesians 4:32)

Practical Applications for Today

Embracing Restorative Practices

The principles demonstrated in Paul's letter to Philemon can be applied in contemporary church settings to promote restorative justice.

1. Reconciliation Ministries: Churches can establish ministries focused on reconciliation, helping members resolve conflicts and restore broken relationships.

Blessed are the peacemakers, for they will be called children of God. (Matthew 5:9)

2. Forgiveness and Support: Encouraging a culture of forgiveness and support within the church can help create a community that reflects Christ's love and grace.

Bear with each other and forgive one another if any of you has a grievance against someone. Forgive as the Lord forgave you. (Colossians 3:13)

Challenging Social Norms

Just as Paul challenged the social norms of his time, contemporary Christians are called to address and challenge injustices within society.

1. Advocacy and Justice: Churches can engage in advocacy and justice work, addressing issues such as inequality, discrimination, and exploitation.

Speak up for those who cannot speak for themselves, for the rights of all who are destitute. (Proverbs 31:8)

2. Inclusive Community: By creating an inclusive community that values each individual, regardless of their background, the church can be a powerful witness to the transformative power of the gospel.

Accept one another, then, just as Christ accepted you, in order to bring praise to God. (Romans 15:7)

The letter to Philemon provides a compelling example of restorative justice in action, demonstrating the power of the gospel to transform lives and relationships. Paul's appeal for Onesimus highlights the principles of grace, forgiveness, and reconciliation, offering a model for how these values can be lived out in the Christian community.

By embracing restorative practices and challenging social norms, contemporary churches can reflect the heart of the gospel and create communities that promote justice, mercy, and reconciliation. As we continue to study Paul's writings and apply their teachings, we can build a church that embodies the principles of restorative justice, fostering environments where individuals are valued, relationships are healed, and God's love is made manifest.

THE RELATIONSHIP BETWEEN PHILEMON, ONESIMUS, AND PAUL

The letter to Philemon is one of the most personal and intimate epistles of the Apostle Paul. It provides a unique glimpse into the relationships between Paul, Philemon, and Onesimus. Understanding these relationships is crucial for grasping the depth of the themes of grace, forgiveness, and restorative justice that Paul advocates. This chapter explores the dynamics between Philemon, Onesimus, and Paul, highlighting the transformative power of the gospel in reshaping personal relationships and social structures.

Philemon: A Leader and Host

Philemon's Role in the Church

Philemon was a wealthy Christian and a leader in the church that met in his home in Colossae. His commitment to the faith and his hospitality towards fellow believers are well-documented in Paul's letter.

1. Faith and Love: Paul commends Philemon for his faith in Jesus Christ and his love for all the saints.

I always thank my God as I remember you in my prayers because I hear about your love for all his holy people and your faith in the Lord Jesus. (Philemon 1:4-5)

2. Host of the Church: As the host of a house church, Philemon played a significant role in the early Christian community, providing a place for worship, fellowship, and teaching.

To Philemon our dear friend and fellow worker— also to Apphia our sister and Archippus our fellow soldier— and to the church that meets in your home. (Philemon 1:1-2)

Philemon's Relationship with Paul

Philemon had a close and respectful relationship with Paul, characterized by mutual respect and partnership in the gospel.

1. Fellow Worker: Paul refers to Philemon as a "dear friend and fellow worker," indicating a partnership in ministry and a shared commitment to spreading the gospel.

To Philemon our dear friend and fellow worker. (Philemon 1:1)

2. Influence and Respect: Paul's respectful and tactful approach in the letter suggests a deep mutual respect. He

appeals to Philemon's sense of Christian duty and love rather than commanding him.

Therefore, although in Christ I could be bold and order you to do what you ought to do, yet I prefer to appeal to you on the basis of love. (Philemon 1:8-9)

Onesimus: The Runaway Slave Turned Brother

Onesimus' Background

Onesimus was a slave belonging to Philemon who had run away, possibly after wronging his master. His encounter with Paul led to a significant transformation in his life.

1. Runaway Slave: Onesimus had fled from Philemon, an act that was both illegal and punishable under Roman law. His status as a fugitive made his situation precarious.

Formerly he was useless to you, but now he has become useful both to you and to me. (Philemon 1:11)

2. Conversion to Christianity: After meeting Paul, Onesimus converted to Christianity. This change in his spiritual status is central to Paul's appeal for his reconciliation with Philemon.

I appeal to you for my son Onesimus, who became my son while I was in chains. (Philemon 1:10)

Onesimus' Relationship with Paul

Onesimus developed a close and affectionate relationship with Paul, who became his spiritual father and advocate.

1. Spiritual Son: Paul describes Onesimus as his son, indicating a deep personal bond and spiritual mentorship.

I appeal to you for my son Onesimus. (Philemon 1:10)

2. Useful and Beloved: Paul plays on the meaning of Onesimus' name, which means "useful," to highlight his transformation and newfound value both to Paul and potentially to Philemon.

Formerly he was useless to you, but now he has become useful both to you and to me. (Philemon 1:11)

3. Paul's Advocate: Paul acts as an advocate for Onesimus, interceding on his behalf and appealing to Philemon for his acceptance and forgiveness.

I am sending him—who is my very heart—back to you. (Philemon 1:12)

Paul's Role as Mediator and Advocate

Paul's Mediating Role

Paul's role in the relationship between Philemon and Onesimus is that of a mediator and advocate. He seeks to bridge the gap between them, promoting reconciliation and restorative justice.

1. Intercession: Paul intercedes on behalf of Onesimus, asking Philemon to forgive him and accept him back not as a slave but as a brother in Christ.

So if you consider me a partner, welcome him as you would welcome me. (Philemon 1:17)

2. Restorative Justice: Paul's appeal emphasizes the principles of restorative justice, focusing on healing and restoring relationships rather than seeking retribution.

Perhaps the reason he was separated from you for a little while was that you might have him back forever— no longer as a slave, but better than a slave, as a dear brother. (Philemon 1:15-16)

Paul's Personal Appeal

Paul uses his personal relationship with Philemon to appeal for Onesimus, leveraging their friendship and Philemon's respect for him.

1. Personal Connection: Paul's appeal is deeply personal, rooted in his close relationship with both Philemon and Onesimus.

I could be bold and order you to do what you ought to do, yet I prefer to appeal to you on the basis of love. (Philemon 1:8-9)

2. Sacrificial Offer: Paul goes so far as to offer to pay any debt Onesimus owes to Philemon, underscoring his commitment to their reconciliation.

If he has done you any wrong or owes you anything, charge it to me. I, Paul, am writing this with my own hand. I will pay it back—not to mention that you owe me your very self. (Philemon 1:18-19)

The Transformative Power of the Gospel

Breaking Social Barriers

The letter to Philemon illustrates how the gospel breaks down social barriers and transforms relationships.

1. New Creation in Christ: The transformation of Onesimus from a slave to a beloved brother in Christ exemplifies the new creation that believers become through faith.

Therefore, if anyone is in Christ, the new creation has come: The old has gone, the new is here! (2 Corinthians 5:17)

2. Equality in Christ: Paul's appeal challenges the social norms of slavery, promoting the idea of equality and brotherhood among all believers.

Here there is no Gentile or Jew, circumcised or uncircumcised, barbarian, Scythian, slave or free, but Christ is all, and is in all. (Colossians 3:11)

Forgiveness and Reconciliation

The letter emphasizes the importance of forgiveness and reconciliation as central themes of the Christian faith.

1. Forgiveness: Paul's request for Philemon to forgive Onesimus reflects the broader Christian imperative to forgive as we have been forgiven by God.

Bear with each other and forgive one another if any of you has a grievance against someone. Forgive as the Lord forgave you. (Colossians 3:13)

2. Reconciliation: The goal of Paul's appeal is not just forgiveness but the complete reconciliation and restoration of the relationship between Philemon and Onesimus.

All this is from God, who reconciled us to Himself through Christ and gave us the ministry of reconciliation. (2 Corinthians 5:18)

Practical Applications for Today

Embracing Restorative Justice

The principles demonstrated in the relationships between Philemon, Onesimus, and Paul can be applied in contemporary church settings to promote restorative justice.

1. Mediation and Reconciliation: Churches can establish mediation and reconciliation ministries to help members resolve conflicts and restore broken relationships.

Blessed are the peacemakers, for they will be called children of God. (Matthew 5:9)

2. Support and Advocacy: Just as Paul advocated for Onesimus, churches can support and advocate for individuals seeking forgiveness and restoration.

Carry each other's burdens, and in this way you will fulfill the law of Christ. (Galatians 6:2)

Challenging Social Norms and Injustices

Paul's letter challenges contemporary Christians to address and challenge social injustices within their own contexts.

1. Equality and Inclusion: Churches should strive to create inclusive communities that value each individual regardless of their social or economic status.

Accept one another, then, just as Christ accepted you, in order to bring praise to God. (Romans 15:7)

2. Advocacy for Justice: Christians are called to advocate for justice and equity, addressing systemic issues of inequality and exploitation.

Speak up for those who cannot speak for themselves, for the rights of all who are destitute. (Proverbs 31:8)

The relationships between Philemon, Onesimus, and Paul provide a powerful example of the transformative power of the gospel in personal relationships and social structures. Through this personal and heartfelt letter, Paul demonstrates the principles

of grace, forgiveness, and restorative justice, challenging the social norms of his time and promoting a vision of equality and brotherhood in Christ.

By embracing these principles and applying them in contemporary settings, churches can foster communities that reflect the heart of the gospel, where justice and mercy prevail, and relationships are healed and restored. As we continue to study Paul's writings and apply their teachings, we can build a church that embodies the transformative power of the gospel, promoting justice, mercy, and reconciliation in all aspects of life.

PAUL'S APPEAL FOR RECONCILIATION AND RESTORATION

Apostle Paul's letter to Philemon is a compelling example of his advocacy for reconciliation and restoration within the Christian community. This personal and heartfelt appeal demonstrates how Paul applies the principles of grace, forgiveness, and restorative justice to real-life situations. This chapter explores Paul's appeal for reconciliation and restoration in the letter to Philemon, examining the theological foundations, practical implications, and the transformative power of the gospel in reshaping relationships.

The Context of the Appeal

Philemon and Onesimus

The relationship between Philemon and Onesimus is at the heart of Paul's appeal. Understanding their background provides essential context for the letter.

1. Philemon: A wealthy Christian and leader in the church at Colossae, Philemon was known for his faith and love towards Jesus and the Christian community.

I always thank my God as I remember you in my prayers because I hear about your love for all his holy people and your faith in the Lord Jesus. (Philemon 1:4-5)

2. Onesimus: A slave who had run away from Philemon, Onesimus encountered Paul and converted to Christianity. His name means "useful," which Paul uses to highlight his transformation.

Formerly he was useless to you, but now he has become useful both to you and to me. (Philemon 1:11)

Paul's Role

Paul acts as a mediator between Philemon and Onesimus, advocating for reconciliation and restoration based on their new relationship in Christ.

1. Spiritual Father: Paul had become a spiritual father to Onesimus, mentoring him and witnessing his transformation.

I appeal to you for my son Onesimus, who became my son while I was in chains. (Philemon 1:10)

2. Partner in Faith: Paul's relationship with Philemon was marked by mutual respect and partnership in the gospel.

So if you consider me a partner, welcome him as you would welcome me. (Philemon 1:17)

The Appeal for Reconciliation

Personal and Respectful Approach

Paul's approach in appealing to Philemon is marked by tact, respect, and a deep sense of Christian love and fellowship.

1. Gentle Appeal: Paul prefers to appeal on the basis of love rather than using his apostolic authority to command Philemon.

Therefore, although in Christ I could be bold and order you to do what you ought to do, yet I prefer to appeal to you on the basis of love. (Philemon 1:8-9)

2. Acknowledging Philemon's Character: Paul acknowledges Philemon's love and faith, building on their relationship to make his appeal more persuasive.

Your love has given me great joy and encouragement, because you, brother, have refreshed the hearts of the Lord's people. (Philemon 1:7)

Emphasizing Onesimus' Transformation

Paul highlights the transformation in Onesimus' life, emphasizing his new identity and usefulness in the Christian community.

1. From Useless to Useful: Paul plays on the meaning of Onesimus' name to illustrate his transformation from a runaway slave to a valuable member of the community.

Formerly he was useless to you, but now he has become useful both to you and to me. (Philemon 1:11)

2. A Beloved Brother: Paul urges Philemon to receive Onesimus not as a slave but as a beloved brother in Christ.

Perhaps the reason he was separated from you for a little while was that you might have him back forever— no longer as a slave, but better than a slave, as a dear brother. (Philemon 1:15-16)

Theological Foundations of the Appeal

Paul's appeal for reconciliation is deeply rooted in the theological principles of grace, forgiveness, and the transformative power of the gospel.

1. New Identity in Christ: Paul emphasizes that in Christ, social barriers are broken down, and believers are united as equals.

Here there is no Gentile or Jew, circumcised or uncircumcised, barbarian, Scythian, slave or free, but Christ is all, and is in all. (Colossians 3:11)

2. Grace and Forgiveness: Paul's request for Philemon to forgive Onesimus reflects the broader Christian imperative to forgive as God has forgiven us.

Bear with each other and forgive one another if any of you has a grievance against someone. Forgive as the Lord forgave you. (Colossians 3:13)

The Appeal for Restoration

Practical Steps for Restoration

Paul provides practical steps for Philemon to restore his relationship with Onesimus, emphasizing the importance of welcoming him back into the community.

1. Welcoming Onesimus: Paul asks Philemon to welcome Onesimus as he would welcome Paul himself, indicating a complete restoration of the relationship.

So if you consider me a partner, welcome him as you would welcome me. (Philemon 1:17)

2. Assuming the Debt: Paul offers to assume any debt Onesimus might owe, demonstrating his commitment to their reconciliation.

If he has done you any wrong or owes you anything, charge it to me. I, Paul, am writing this with my own hand. I will pay it back—not to mention that you owe me your very self. (Philemon 1:18-19)

Long-Term Implications

Paul's appeal has long-term implications for the relationships within the Christian community and the broader social structure.

1. Model of Christian Brotherhood: The reconciliation between Philemon and Onesimus serves as a model for Christian brotherhood and equality, challenging the existing social norms.

Therefore, if anyone is in Christ, the new creation has come: The old has gone, the new is here! (2 Corinthians 5:17)

2. Community Witness: The act of reconciliation would serve as a powerful witness to the transformative power of the gospel, demonstrating the values of grace, forgiveness, and unity.

By this everyone will know that you are my disciples if you love one another. (John 13:35)

Practical Applications for Today

Embracing Restorative Practices

The principles demonstrated in Paul's appeal can be applied in contemporary church settings to promote restorative justice.

1. Reconciliation Ministries: Churches can establish reconciliation ministries to help members resolve conflicts and restore broken relationships.

Blessed are the peacemakers, for they will be called children of God. (Matthew 5:9)

2. Forgiveness and Support: Encouraging a culture of forgiveness and support within the church can help create a community that reflects Christ's love and grace.

Bear with each other and forgive one another if any of you has a grievance against someone. Forgive as the Lord forgave you. (Colossians 3:13)

Challenging Social Norms

Paul's letter challenges contemporary Christians to address and challenge social injustices within their own contexts.

1. Equality and Inclusion: Churches should strive to create inclusive communities that value each individual regardless of their social or economic status.

Accept one another, then, just as Christ accepted you, in order to bring praise to God. (Romans 15:7)

2. Advocacy for Justice: Christians are called to advocate for justice and equity, addressing systemic issues of inequality and exploitation.

Speak up for those who cannot speak for themselves, for the rights of all who are destitute. (Proverbs 31:8)

Paul's appeal for reconciliation and restoration in the letter to Philemon provides a powerful example of the transformative power of the gospel in personal relationships and social structures. By advocating for Onesimus and appealing to Philemon's sense of Christian duty and love, Paul demonstrates the principles of grace, forgiveness, and restorative justice.

These principles are not only relevant for the early Christian community but also for contemporary churches seeking to embody the values of the gospel. By embracing restorative practices, challenging social norms, and promoting equality and inclusion, the church can reflect the heart of the gospel and create communities where justice and mercy prevail.

As we continue to study Paul's writings and apply their teachings, we can build a church that embodies the transformative power of the gospel, promoting justice, mercy, and reconciliation in all aspects of life.

LESSONS FOR MODERN RESTORATIVE JUSTICE PRACTICES

The letter to Philemon stands as a timeless testament to the principles of grace, forgiveness, and reconciliation, serving as a rich source of lessons for modern restorative justice practices. This chapter draws from Paul's appeal to Philemon, identifying key lessons that can be applied to contemporary settings to promote restorative justice within communities, organizations, and societies at large.

Understanding Restorative Justice in Philemon

Core Principles

Restorative justice focuses on repairing harm, restoring relationships, and reintegrating offenders into the community. The letter to Philemon exemplifies these principles in several key ways:

1. Reconciliation Over Retribution: Paul's appeal centers on reconciliation rather than punishment, urging Philemon to forgive Onesimus and accept him as a brother.

Perhaps the reason he was separated from you for a little while was that you might have him back forever— no longer as a slave, but better than a slave, as a dear brother. (Philemon 1:15-16)

2. Personal Transformation: Paul highlights Onesimus's transformation through his faith in Christ, emphasizing the potential for personal change and redemption.

I appeal to you for my son Onesimus, who became my son while I was in chains. (Philemon 1:10)

3. Community Involvement: The letter underscores the importance of the community's role in the restorative process, with Paul, Philemon, and Onesimus each playing crucial parts.

So if you consider me a partner, welcome him as you would welcome me. (Philemon 1:17)

Lessons for Modern Restorative Justice Practices

Emphasizing Reconciliation

One of the fundamental lessons from Paul's letter is the importance of prioritizing reconciliation over retribution.

1. Creating Opportunities for Forgiveness: Modern restorative justice practices should create opportunities for victims and offenders to engage in dialogue, express their feelings, and seek forgiveness.

If your brother or sister sins against you, go and point out their fault, just between the two of you. If they listen to you, you have won them over. (Matthew 18:15)

2.   Fostering   Understanding: Encouraging understanding and empathy between parties can help heal wounds and restore relationships, much like Paul's appeal for Philemon to understand Onesimus's transformation.

Bear with each other and forgive one another if any of you has a grievance against someone. Forgive as the Lord forgave you. (Colossians 3:13)

Encouraging Personal Transformation

Paul's focus on Onesimus's personal transformation highlights the potential for individuals to change and the importance of supporting this process.

1. Supporting Rehabilitation: Modern practices should include support systems that aid offenders in their rehabilitation and reintegration into society.

Carry each other's burdens, and in this way you will fulfill the law of Christ. (Galatians 6:2)

2. Highlighting Positive Change: Recognizing and celebrating the positive changes in individuals can reinforce their commitment to transformation and inspire others.

Therefore, if anyone is in Christ, the new creation has come: The old has gone, the new is here! (2 Corinthians 5:17)

Involving the Community

The involvement of the community in the restorative process is crucial, as demonstrated by Paul's role in mediating between Philemon and Onesimus.

1. Community Mediation Programs: Establishing community-based mediation programs can provide neutral spaces where conflicts can be resolved through dialogue and mutual agreement.

Blessed are the peacemakers, for they will be called children of God. (Matthew 5:9)

2. Building Support Networks: Creating support networks within the community can help both victims and offenders receive the emotional, social, and spiritual support they need.

Encourage one another and build each other up, just as in fact you are doing. (1 Thessalonians 5:11)

Practicing Restorative Discipline

Paul's approach to resolving the conflict between Philemon and Onesimus provides a model for practicing restorative discipline within modern institutions.

1. Fair and Compassionate Processes: Ensuring that disciplinary processes are fair and compassionate, focusing on repairing harm rather than merely punishing the offender.

Brothers and sisters, if someone is caught in a sin, you who live by the Spirit should restore that person gently.

But watch yourselves, or you also may be tempted. (Galatians 6:1)

2. Clear Pathways to Restoration: Providing clear pathways for offenders to be restored to the community, including opportunities for making amends and demonstrating repentance.

If we confess our sins, he is faithful and just and will forgive us our sins and purify us from all unrighteousness. (1 John 1:9)

Practical Applications in Contemporary Settings

Restorative Justice in the Criminal Justice System

Applying the principles from Philemon to the criminal justice system can transform how justice is administered.

1. Victim-Offender Mediation: Implementing victim-offender mediation programs where victims and offenders can discuss the impact of the crime and agree on steps for restitution.

The Lord is close to the brokenhearted and saves those who are crushed in spirit. (Psalm 34:18)

2. Restorative Circles: Using restorative circles to involve the community in the justice process, providing a space for collective healing and support.

If one part suffers, every part suffers with it; if one part is honored, every part rejoices with it. (1 Corinthians 12:26)

Restorative Practices in Schools

Schools can benefit from restorative practices by fostering a culture of respect, responsibility, and community.

1. Peer Mediation Programs: Establishing peer mediation programs where students are trained to help their peers resolve conflicts peacefully.

Let us therefore make every effort to do what leads to peace and to mutual edification. (Romans 14:19)

2. Restorative Discipline: Implementing restorative discipline policies that focus on repairing harm and restoring relationships rather than punitive measures.

Fathers, do not exasperate your children; instead, bring them up in the training and instruction of the Lord. (Ephesians 6:4)

Restorative Practices in Workplaces

Workplaces can create healthier and more productive environments by incorporating restorative practices.

1. Conflict Resolution Programs: Developing conflict resolution programs that encourage open dialogue and mutual understanding between employees.

Do not repay anyone evil for evil. Be careful to do what is right in the eyes of everyone. If it is possible, as far as it depends on you, live at peace with everyone. (Romans 12:17-18)

2. Employee Support Networks: Creating support networks within the workplace to help employees navigate conflicts and personal challenges.

Carry each other's burdens, and in this way you will fulfill the law of Christ. (Galatians 6:2)

Challenges and Considerations

Addressing Resistance to Restorative Practices

Implementing restorative practices can face resistance from those accustomed to traditional punitive approaches.

1. Education and Training: Providing education and training on the benefits and principles of restorative justice can help overcome resistance and build support.

All Scripture is God-breathed and is useful for teaching, rebuking, correcting and training in righteousness. (2 Timothy 3:16)

2. Leadership Support: Gaining the support of leaders and influencers within the community or organization can facilitate the adoption of restorative practices.

Remember your leaders, who spoke the word of God to you. Consider the outcome of their way of life and imitate their faith. (Hebrews 13:7)

Ensuring Fairness and Equity

Ensuring that restorative practices are applied fairly and equitably is essential for their success.

1. Inclusive Processes: Designing processes that are inclusive and accessible to all members of the community, regardless of their background or status.

My brothers and sisters, believers in our glorious Lord Jesus Christ must not show favoritism. (James 2:1)

2. Monitoring and Evaluation: Regularly monitoring and evaluating restorative practices to ensure they are effective and fair, making adjustments as needed.

Examine yourselves to see whether you are in the faith; test yourselves. Do you not realize that Christ Jesus is in you—unless, of course, you fail the test? (2 Corinthians 13:5)

The letter to Philemon provides a powerful example of restorative justice in action, demonstrating the principles of reconciliation, personal transformation, and community involvement. By applying these principles to contemporary settings, we can create communities and institutions that prioritize healing, forgiveness, and restoration over punishment and retribution.

Implementing restorative practices in the criminal justice system, schools, workplaces, and other areas can transform how we address conflicts and harm, promoting a culture of respect, responsibility, and mutual support. Overcoming resistance and ensuring fairness and equity are essential for the success of these practices, requiring ongoing education, support, and evaluation.

As we continue to draw lessons from Paul's writings and the example of Philemon, we can build a more just and compassionate society, reflecting the transformative power of the gospel in all aspects of life.

CHAPTER 08

THE ROLE OF LOVE IN RESTORATIVE JUSTICE

The theology of Apostle Paul is profoundly centered on love, which he presents as the highest virtue and the foundation of all Christian ethics. Paul's teachings on love, particularly in passages like 1 Corinthians 13 and Romans 13:8-10, provide a crucial framework for understanding and practicing restorative justice. This chapter explores Paul's theology of love and examines how it informs and enhances restorative justice practices.

Paul's Theology of Love

Love as the Greatest Virtue

In 1 Corinthians 13, Paul offers a detailed exposition on the nature and importance of love, emphasizing its supremacy over all other spiritual gifts and virtues.

1. The Supremacy of Love: Paul declares that without love, all other gifts and actions are meaningless.

If I speak in the tongues of men or of angels, but do not have love, I am only a resounding gong or a clanging cymbal. (1 Corinthians 13:1)

2. Characteristics of Love: Paul describes love's qualities, highlighting its patience, kindness, and endurance.

Love is patient, love is kind. It does not envy, it does not boast, it is not proud. It does not dishonor others, it is not self-seeking, it is not easily angered, and it keeps no record of wrongs. (1 Corinthians 13:4-5)

3. Permanence of Love: Unlike other gifts that will pass away, love endures forever, making it the greatest virtue.

And now these three remain faith, hope, and love. But the greatest of these is love. (1 Corinthians 13:13)

Love Fulfills the Law

In Romans 13:8-10, Paul connects love with the fulfillment of the law, underscoring its foundational role in Christian life and ethics.

1. Debt of Love: Paul encourages believers to owe nothing except love to one another, presenting love as an ongoing obligation.

Let no debt remain outstanding, except the continuing debt to love one another, for whoever loves others has fulfilled the law. (Romans 13:8)

2. Love and the Commandments: Paul states that all commandments are summed up in the command to love one's neighbor as oneself.

The commandments, "You shall not commit adultery," "You shall not murder," "You shall not steal," "You shall not covet," and whatever other command there may be, are summed up in this one command: "Love your neighbor as yourself." (Romans 13:9)

3. Love and Harm: Love does no harm to a neighbor, thus fulfilling the law.

Love does no harm to a neighbor. Therefore love is the fulfillment of the law. (Romans 13:10)

Love as the Foundation of Restorative Justice

The Motivating Force

Love serves as the motivating force behind restorative justice, driving the desire to heal and restore rather than punish.

1. Compassion and Empathy: Restorative justice is rooted in compassion and empathy, seeking to understand and address the needs of all parties involved.

Be kind and compassionate to one another, forgiving each other, just as in Christ God forgave you. (Ephesians 4:32)

2. Reconciliation and Healing: The goal of restorative justice is to reconcile and heal relationships, reflecting the reconciling love of Christ.

All this is from God, who reconciled us to himself through Christ and gave us the ministry of reconciliation. (2 Corinthians 5:18)

The Guiding Principle

Love guides the actions and decisions within restorative justice, ensuring that they are fair, just, and compassionate.

1. Non-Retaliation: Love rejects retaliation and seeks to break the cycle of harm by responding with forgiveness and understanding.

Do not repay anyone evil for evil. Be careful to do what is right in the eyes of everyone. (Romans 12:17)

2. Active Goodness: Love actively seeks the good of others, promoting practices that build up and support all individuals involved.

Do not be overcome by evil, but overcome evil with good. (Romans 12:21)

Practical Applications of Love in Restorative Justice

Creating Safe and Supportive Environments

Love-driven restorative justice practices create safe and supportive environments for dialogue and healing.

1. Safe Spaces for Dialogue: Establishing safe spaces where victims and offenders can share their stories and feelings without fear of judgment or retribution.

Speak the truth in love, and we will grow to become in every respect the mature body of him who is the head, that is, Christ. (Ephesians 4:15)

2. Support Systems: Providing emotional and practical support for both victims and offenders to facilitate healing and reintegration.

Carry each other's burdens, and in this way you will fulfill the law of Christ. (Galatians 6:2)

Emphasizing Forgiveness and Reconciliation

Forgiveness and reconciliation are central to love-driven restorative justice, aiming to restore broken relationships.

1. Promoting Forgiveness: Encouraging forgiveness as a path to healing and freedom from bitterness and resentment.

Bear with each other and forgive one another if any of you has a grievance against someone. Forgive as the Lord forgave you. (Colossians 3:13)

2. Facilitating Reconciliation: Implementing processes that facilitate reconciliation, allowing for honest communication, repentance, and restoration.

If it is possible, as far as it depends on you, live at peace with everyone. (Romans 12:18)

Restorative Practices in Action

Implementing restorative practices that reflect the principles of love can transform how justice is administered.

1. Restorative Circles: Using restorative circles to bring together victims, offenders, and community members to discuss the harm caused and agree on steps for making amends.

Therefore, if you are offering your gift at the altar and remember that your brother or sister has something against you, leave your gift there in front of the altar. First, go and be reconciled to them; then come and offer your gift. (Matthew 5:23-24)

2. Victim-Offender Mediation: Facilitating mediation sessions where victims and offenders can engage in constructive dialogue, leading to mutual understanding and agreements on restitution.

Blessed are the peacemakers, for they will be called children of God. (Matthew 5:9)

Challenges and Considerations

Balancing Love and Justice

One of the primary challenges in restorative justice is balancing the need for justice with the imperative of love.

1. Ensuring Fairness: While prioritizing love and compassion, it is essential to ensure that justice is fairly administered, and the needs of victims are adequately addressed.

But let justice roll on like a river, righteousness like a never-failing stream! (Amos 5:24)

2. Avoiding Enabling: Ensuring that the focus on love and forgiveness does not enable harmful behavior but promotes genuine accountability and transformation.

If we confess our sins, he is faithful and just and will forgive us our sins and purify us from all unrighteousness. (1 John 1:9)

Cultivating a Culture of Love

Creating a culture of love within communities and institutions is essential for the success of restorative justice practices.

1. Leadership and Example: Leaders should model the principles of love and restorative justice, setting an example for others to follow.

Follow my example, as I follow the example of Christ. (1 Corinthians 11:1)

2. Education and Training: Providing education and training on the principles of love and restorative justice can help cultivate a culture that supports these practices.

And the things you have heard me say in the presence of many witnesses entrust to reliable people who will also be qualified to teach others. (2 Timothy 2:2)

Paul's theology of love, as articulated in passages like 1 Corinthians 13 and Romans 13:8-10, provides a profound foundation for restorative justice practices. Love serves as both the motivating force and guiding principle, driving the desire to heal and restore relationships and ensuring that actions are fair, just, and compassionate.

By creating safe and supportive environments, emphasizing forgiveness and reconciliation, and implementing restorative practices, modern restorative justice can reflect the transformative power of love. Balancing love and justice and cultivating a culture of love are essential for the success of these practices, requiring ongoing commitment and leadership.

As we continue to draw lessons from Paul's writings, we can build communities and institutions that embody the principles of love and restorative justice, promoting healing, reconciliation, and the flourishing of all individuals.

LOVE AS THE FOUNDATION FOR JUSTICE AND RECONCILIATION

In the theology of Apostle Paul, love is not merely an emotional response but the bedrock of Christian ethics and community life. Love underpins justice and reconciliation, guiding believers in their interactions and shaping the ethos of the church. This chapter explores how Paul presents love as the foundation for justice and reconciliation, examining key biblical texts and their implications for contemporary practice.

Paul's Theology of Love

Love as the Greatest Commandment

Paul's understanding of love is deeply rooted in Jesus' teaching that the greatest commandment is to love God and love one's neighbor.

1. The Centrality of Love: Paul emphasizes that love is the most important virtue, without which all other actions are meaningless.

If I speak in the tongues of men or of angels, but do not have love, I am only a resounding gong or a clanging cymbal. (1 Corinthians 13:1)

2. Love Summarizes the Law: For Paul, love encapsulates the essence of the law and prophets, guiding ethical behavior and interpersonal relationships.

The commandments, "You shall not commit adultery," "You shall not murder," "You shall not steal," "You shall not covet," and whatever other command there may be, are summed up in this one command: "Love your neighbor as yourself." (Romans 13:9)

Characteristics of Love

Paul's detailed description of love in 1 Corinthians 13 provides a blueprint for how love should manifest in the lives of believers.

1. Patience and Kindness: Love is marked by patience and kindness, reflecting a commitment to the well-being of others.

Love is patient, love is kind. (1 Corinthians 13:4)

2. Selflessness: True love is selfless, putting the needs and interests of others above one's own.

It does not dishonor others, it is not self-seeking, it is not easily angered, it keeps no record of wrongs. (1 Corinthians 13:5)

3. Perseverance: Love endures through difficulties, remaining steadfast and faithful.

It always protects, always trusts, always hopes, always perseveres. (1 Corinthians 13:7)

Love and Justice

Love Motivates Justice

Paul's writings reveal that love is the driving force behind the pursuit of justice. Love compels believers to seek fairness and equity in their relationships and communities.

1. Justice as an Expression of Love: Pursuing justice is an act of love, as it seeks to uphold the dignity and rights of every individual.

Do not repay anyone evil for evil. Be careful to do what is right in the eyes of everyone. (Romans 12:17)

2. Protection of the Vulnerable: Love motivates the protection of the vulnerable and marginalized, ensuring that justice is served.

Defend the weak and the fatherless; uphold the cause of the poor and the oppressed. (Psalm 82:3)

Love Guides Justice

Love shapes how justice is administered, ensuring that it is carried out with compassion and a desire for restoration rather than retribution.

1. Restorative Justice: Justice rooted in love seeks to restore relationships and repair harm rather than simply punish.

Brothers and sisters, if someone is caught in a sin, you who live by the Spirit should restore that person gently. But watch yourselves, or you also may be tempted. (Galatians 6:1)

2. Merciful Justice: Love-infused justice is merciful, taking into account the circumstances and potential for redemption.

Because judgment without mercy will be shown to anyone who has not been merciful. Mercy triumphs over judgment. (James 2:13)

Love and Reconciliation

Love Facilitates Reconciliation

Paul's epistles demonstrate that love is essential for reconciliation, healing divisions, and fostering unity within the church.

1. Forgiveness: Love drives the willingness to forgive, which is a critical step in the process of reconciliation.

Bear with each other and forgive one another if any of you has a grievance against someone. Forgive as the Lord forgave you. (Colossians 3:13)

2. Peacemaking: Love inspires believers to act as peacemakers, seeking to resolve conflicts and restore harmony.

Blessed are the peacemakers, for they will be called children of God. (Matthew 5:9)

Love Builds Community

Paul's vision of the church as a loving community underscores the role of love in creating a supportive and inclusive environment.

1. Unity in Diversity: Love fosters unity in diversity, encouraging acceptance and mutual respect among believers.

So in Christ Jesus you are all children of God through faith. There is neither Jew nor Gentile, neither slave nor free, nor is there male and female, for you are all one in Christ Jesus. (Galatians 3:26, 28)

2. Mutual Support: Love prompts believers to support one another, bearing each other's burdens and working together for the common good.

Carry each other's burdens, and in this way you will fulfill the law of Christ. (Galatians 6:2)

Practical Applications for Today

Building Loving Communities

Churches and communities can apply Paul's teachings on love to build environments that reflect the principles of justice and reconciliation.

1. Promoting Inclusivity: Ensuring that all members feel valued and included, regardless of their background or status.

Accept one another, then, just as Christ accepted you, in order to bring praise to God. (Romans 15:7)

2. Encouraging Forgiveness: Creating a culture that encourages forgiveness and reconciliation, providing opportunities for dialogue and healing.

If your brother or sister sins against you, go and point out their fault, just between the two of you. If they listen to you, you have won them over. (Matthew 18:15)

Implementing Restorative Practices

Restorative practices that are grounded in love can transform how justice is administered in various settings, from churches to schools to workplaces.

1. Restorative Circles: Using restorative circles to address conflicts and harms, allowing all parties to share their perspectives and agree on steps for making amends.

Therefore, if you are offering your gift at the altar and remember that your brother or sister has something against you, leave your gift there in front of the altar. First, go and be reconciled to them; then come and offer your gift. (Matthew 5:23-24)

2. Victim-Offender Mediation: Facilitating mediation sessions where victims and offenders can engage in constructive dialogue, leading to mutual understanding and agreements on restitution.

Blessed are the peacemakers, for they will be called children of God. (Matthew 5:9)

Advocating for Justice

Believers are called to advocate for justice in their communities, driven by the love of Christ.

1. Standing Up for the Oppressed: Actively working to address injustices and support those who are marginalized and oppressed.

Speak up for those who cannot speak for themselves, for the rights of all who are destitute. (Proverbs 31:8)

2. Promoting Fairness and Equity: Ensuring that systems and institutions operate fairly, providing equal opportunities and treatment for all individuals.

Learn to do right; seek justice. Defend the oppressed. Take up the cause of the fatherless; plead the case of the widow. (Isaiah 1:17)

Challenges and Considerations

Overcoming Resistance

Implementing love-driven justice and reconciliation can face resistance from those accustomed to traditional punitive approaches.

1. Education and Training: Providing education and training on the benefits and principles of restorative justice can help overcome resistance and build support.

All Scripture is God-breathed and is useful for teaching, rebuking, correcting and training in righteousness. (2 Timothy 3:16)

2. Leadership Support: Gaining the support of leaders and influencers within the community or organization can facilitate the adoption of restorative practices.

Remember your leaders, who spoke the word of God to you. Consider the outcome of their way of life and imitate their faith. (Hebrews 13:7)

Maintaining Balance

Balancing love with justice and reconciliation requires ongoing attention and intentionality.

1. Ensuring Fairness: While prioritizing love and compassion, it is essential to ensure that justice is fairly administered, and the needs of victims are adequately addressed.

But let justice roll on like a river, righteousness like a never-failing stream! (Amos 5:24)

2. Avoiding Enabling: Ensuring that the focus on love and forgiveness does not enable harmful behavior but promotes genuine accountability and transformation.

If we confess our sins, he is faithful and just and will forgive us our sins and purify us from all unrighteousness. (1 John 1:9)

Paul's theology of love provides a powerful foundation for justice and reconciliation, emphasizing that love is the highest virtue and the guiding principle for all Christian behavior. By grounding justice and reconciliation in love, believers can create communities that reflect the heart of the gospel, promoting healing, unity, and mutual support.

Building loving communities, implementing restorative practices, and advocating for justice are practical ways to live out these principles. Overcoming resistance and maintaining balance is essential for the success of these efforts, requiring ongoing commitment and leadership.

As we continue to draw lessons from Paul's writings, we can build a more just and compassionate society, reflecting the transformative power of love in all aspects of life.

PRACTICAL IMPLICATION FOR RESTORATIVE PRACTICES

Paul's teachings on love, justice, and reconciliation provide a robust theological foundation for restorative practices. These principles, when applied in contemporary settings, can transform how communities address conflict, harm, and justice. This chapter explores the practical implications of implementing restorative practices grounded in Paul's theology, offering guidance for creating environments that foster healing, restoration, and reconciliation.

Understanding Restorative Practices

Defining Restorative Practices

Restorative practices are approaches that focus on repairing harm, restoring relationships, and reintegrating individuals into the community. These practices emphasize accountability, forgiveness, and reconciliation.

1. Repairing Harm: Addressing the needs of those affected by wrongdoing and finding ways to make amends.

If someone is caught in a sin, you who live by the Spirit should restore that person gently. (Galatians 6:1)

2. Restoring Relationships: Rebuilding trust and repairing relationships between the wrongdoer, the victim, and the community.

All this is from God, who reconciled us to himself through Christ and gave us the ministry of reconciliation. (2 Corinthians 5:18)

3. Reintegrating Individuals: Helping offenders reintegrate into the community after making amends, ensuring they are supported and guided.

Carry each other's burdens, and in this way you will fulfill the law of Christ. (Galatians 6:2)

Implementing Restorative Practices

Creating Safe and Supportive Environments

Establishing a safe and supportive environment is crucial for effective restorative practices.

1. Safe Spaces for Dialogue: Creating spaces where individuals can express their feelings and experiences without fear of judgment or retaliation.

Speak the truth in love, and we will grow to become in every respect the mature body of him who is the head, that is, Christ. (Ephesians 4:15)

2. Emotional and Practical Support: Providing emotional and practical support for both victims and offenders, facilitating healing and reintegration.

Carry each other's burdens, and in this way you will fulfill the law of Christ. (Galatians 6:2)

Facilitating Forgiveness and Reconciliation

Forgiveness and reconciliation are central to restorative practices, aiming to heal relationships and restore community harmony.

1. Encouraging Forgiveness: Promoting forgiveness as a key step towards healing and liberation from resentment.

Bear with each other and forgive one another if any of you has a grievance against someone. Forgive as the Lord forgave you. (Colossians 3:13)

2. Structured Reconciliation Processes: Implementing structured processes that facilitate reconciliation, allowing for open communication, repentance, and restoration.

If it is possible, as far as it depends on you, live at peace with everyone. (Romans 12:18)

Restorative Practices in Action

Implementing specific restorative practices can transform how justice and conflict resolution are approached in various settings.

1. Restorative Circles: Using restorative circles to bring together victims, offenders, and community members to discuss the harm caused and agree on steps for making amends.

Therefore, if you are offering your gift at the altar and there remember that your brother or sister has something against you, leave your gift there in front of the altar. First go and be reconciled to them; then come and offer your gift. (Matthew 5:23-24)

2. Victim-Offender Mediation: Facilitating mediation sessions where victims and offenders can engage in constructive dialogue, leading to mutual understanding and agreements on restitution.

Blessed are the peacemakers, for they will be called children of God. (Matthew 5:9)

Applications in Various Contexts

Restorative Justice in the Criminal Justice System

Applying restorative practices in the criminal justice system can lead to more humane and effective outcomes.

1. Victim-Offender Dialogue: Implementing programs that allow victims and offenders to engage in dialogue, promoting healing and understanding.

The Lord is close to the brokenhearted and saves those who are crushed in spirit. (Psalm 34:18)

2. Community Service and Restitution: Encouraging offenders to make amends through community service and restitution, fostering accountability and repair of harm.

If a thief is caught, he must pay back seven times what he stole, even if he has to sell everything in his house. (Proverbs 6:31)

Restorative Practices in Schools

Schools can benefit significantly from restorative practices, creating a positive and supportive learning environment.

1. Peer Mediation Programs: Establishing peer mediation programs where students are trained to help their peers resolve conflicts peacefully.

Let us therefore make every effort to do what leads to peace and to mutual edification. (Romans 14:19)

2. Restorative Discipline: Implementing restorative discipline policies that focus on repairing harm and restoring relationships rather than punitive measures.

Fathers, do not exasperate your children; instead, bring them up in the training and instruction of the Lord. (Ephesians 6:4)

Restorative Practices in Workplaces

Workplaces can create healthier and more productive environments by incorporating restorative practices.

1. Conflict Resolution Programs: Developing conflict resolution programs that encourage open dialogue and mutual understanding between employees.

Do not repay anyone evil for evil. Be careful to do what is right in the eyes of everyone. If it is possible, as far as it depends on you, live at peace with everyone. (Romans 12:17-18)

2. Employee Support Networks: Creating support networks within the workplace to help employees navigate conflicts and personal challenges.

Carry each other's burdens, and in this way you will fulfill the law of Christ. (Galatians 6:2)

Challenges and Considerations

Overcoming Resistance

Implementing restorative practices can face resistance from those accustomed to traditional punitive approaches.

1. Education and Training: Providing education and training on the benefits and principles of restorative justice can help overcome resistance and build support.

All Scripture is God-breathed and is useful for teaching, rebuking, correcting, and training in righteousness. (2 Timothy 3:16)

2. Leadership Support: Gaining the support of leaders and influencers within the community or organization can facilitate the adoption of restorative practices.

Remember your leaders, who spoke the word of God to you. Consider the outcome of their way of life and imitate their faith. (Hebrews 13:7)

Ensuring Fairness and Equity

Ensuring that restorative practices are applied fairly and equitably is essential for their success.

1. Inclusive Processes: Designing processes that are inclusive and accessible to all members of the community, regardless of their background or status.

My brothers and sisters, believers in our glorious Lord Jesus Christ must not show favoritism. (James 2:1)

2. Monitoring and Evaluation: Regularly monitoring and evaluating restorative practices to ensure they are effective and fair, making adjustments as needed.

Examine yourselves to see whether you are in the faith; test yourselves. Do you not realize that Christ Jesus is in you—unless, of course, you fail the test? (2 Corinthians 13:5)

Building a Culture of Restorative Justice

Promoting a Restorative Mindset

Fostering a mindset that values restorative justice is crucial for the successful implementation of these practices.

1. Teaching and Preaching: Regularly teaching and preaching about the principles of restorative justice can help embed these values in the community's culture.

All Scripture is God-breathed and is useful for teaching, rebuking, correcting and training in righteousness. (2 Timothy 3:16)

2. Role Modeling: Leaders and influential members of the community should model restorative practices in their interactions and decision-making processes.

Follow my example, as I follow the example of Christ. (1 Corinthians 11:1)

Encouraging Community Involvement

Community involvement is key to the success of restorative practices, ensuring that everyone has a stake in the process.

1. Collaborative Decision-Making: Involving community members in the decision-making process for implementing restorative practices can foster ownership and commitment.

Plans fail for lack of counsel, but with many advisers, they succeed. (Proverbs 15:22)

2. Building Support Networks: Establishing support networks within the community can provide ongoing support and resources for individuals involved in restorative justice processes.

Carry each other's burdens, and in this way you will fulfill the law of Christ. (Galatians 6:2)

Implementing restorative practices based on Paul's teachings on love, justice, and reconciliation can transform how communities address conflict and harm. By creating safe and supportive environments, facilitating forgiveness and reconciliation, and applying restorative practices in various contexts, communities can promote healing and restoration.

Overcoming resistance and ensuring fairness and equity are essential for the success of these practices, requiring ongoing education, support, and evaluation. By fostering a restorative mindset and encouraging community involvement, communities can build a culture that reflects the heart of the gospel, promoting justice, mercy, and reconciliation.

As we continue to draw lessons from Paul's writings, we can build more just and compassionate societies, reflecting the transformative power of love and restorative justice in all aspects of life.

FOSTERING A CULTURE OF LOVE AND RESTORATION IN THE CHURCH

The teachings of Apostle Paul emphasize the importance of love and restoration as central to the Christian faith. Building a culture of love and restoration within the church involves integrating these principles into every aspect of church life, from interpersonal relationships to organizational structures. This chapter explores practical strategies for fostering such a culture, drawing on Paul's theological insights and practical exhortations.

Understanding the Foundation of Love and Restoration

The Centrality of Love

Paul's epistles underscore that love is the greatest virtue and the foundation of all Christian ethics.

1. Love as the Greatest Commandment: Paul reiterates Jesus' teaching that the greatest commandments are to love God and love one's neighbor.

The commandments, "You shall not commit adultery," "You shall not murder," "You shall not steal," "You shall not covet," and whatever other command there may be, are summed up in this one command: "Love your neighbor as yourself." (Romans 13:9)

2. The Characteristics of Love: In 1 Corinthians 13, Paul provides a detailed description of love's attributes, emphasizing patience, kindness, and humility.

Love is patient, love is kind. It does not envy, it does not boast, it is not proud. It does not dishonor others, it is not self-seeking, it is not easily angered, it keeps no record of wrongs. (1 Corinthians 13:4-5)

The Role of Restoration

Restoration is about mending broken relationships and reintegrating individuals into the community, reflecting God's redemptive work through Christ.

1. Restoration Through Forgiveness: Paul highlights the importance of forgiveness in restoring relationships.

Bear with each other and forgive one another if any of you has a grievance against someone. Forgive as the Lord forgave you. (Colossians 3:13)

2. Reconciliation and Unity: Paul calls believers to pursue reconciliation, aiming to restore unity within the church.

All this is from God, who reconciled us to Himself through Christ and gave us the ministry of reconciliation. (2 Corinthians 5:18)

Building a Culture of Love

Teaching and Preaching on Love

Regular teaching and preaching about the principles of love are essential for embedding these values into the church culture.

1. Biblical Teachings on Love: Preach and teach from scriptures that emphasize love, such as 1 Corinthians 13 and Romans 12.

Love must be sincere. Hate what is evil; cling to what is good. Be devoted to one another in love. Honor one another above yourselves. (Romans 12:9-10)

2. Practical Applications: Provide practical applications of love in everyday life, encouraging members to practice kindness, patience, and humility in their interactions.

Therefore, as God's chosen people, holy and dearly loved, clothe yourselves with compassion, kindness, humility, gentleness, and patience. (Colossians 3:12)

Modeling Love in Leadership

Church leaders play a crucial role in modeling the principles of love and setting the tone for the community.

1. Servant Leadership: Leaders should exemplify servant leadership, prioritizing the needs of others and demonstrating humility.

But among you, it will be different. Whoever wants to be a leader among you must be your servant. (Matthew 20:26)

2. Inclusive and Compassionate: Leaders should be inclusive and compassionate, ensuring that all members feel valued and supported.

Be completely humble and gentle; be patient, bearing with one another in love. (Ephesians 4:2)

Fostering Loving Relationships

Encouraging members to build loving relationships is fundamental to creating a supportive and inclusive church community.

1. Small Groups and Fellowship: Promote small groups and fellowship activities that allow members to build deeper relationships and support one another.

And let us consider how we may spur one another on toward love and good deeds, not giving up meeting together, as some are in the habit of doing, but encouraging one another—and all the more as you see the Day approaching. (Hebrews 10:24-25)

2. Acts of Service: Encourage acts of service within the church and the broader community, fostering a spirit of generosity and care.

Each of you should use whatever gift you have received to serve others, as faithful stewards of God's grace in its various forms. (1 Peter 4:10)

Building a Culture of Restoration

Implementing Restorative Practices

Restorative practices help address conflicts and harm within the church, promoting healing and reconciliation.

1. Restorative Circles: Use restorative circles to address conflicts, allowing all parties to share their experiences and agree on steps for making amends.

Therefore, if you are offering your gift at the altar and there remember that your brother or sister has something against you, leave your gift there in front of the altar. First go and be reconciled to them; then come and offer your gift. (Matthew 5:23-24)

2. Mediation and Counseling: Provide mediation and counseling services to help members navigate conflicts and work towards reconciliation.

Blessed are the peacemakers, for they will be called children of God. (Matthew 5:9)

Encouraging Forgiveness and Reconciliation

Forgiveness and reconciliation are key components of restoration, helping to mend broken relationships and restore unity.

1. Teaching on Forgiveness: Regularly teach about the importance of forgiveness, using biblical examples and practical applications.

Bear with each other and forgive one another if any of you has a grievance against someone. Forgive as the Lord forgave you. (Colossians 3:13)

2. Creating Opportunities for Reconciliation: Create structured opportunities for reconciliation, such as reconciliation services or retreats.

If it is possible, as far as it depends on you, live at peace with everyone. (Romans 12:18)

Supporting Those in Need of Restoration

Provide support for individuals who need restoration, ensuring they have the resources and guidance they need to reintegrate into the community.

1. Support Groups: Establish support groups for individuals dealing with specific issues, such as addiction, grief, or relational conflicts.

Carry each other's burdens, and in this way you will fulfill the law of Christ. (Galatians 6:2)

2. Mentorship Programs: Implement mentorship programs where more mature believers can provide guidance and support to those in need of restoration.

Follow my example, as I follow the example of Christ. (1 Corinthians 11:1)

Overcoming Challenges

Addressing Resistance to Change

Implementing a culture of love and restoration may face resistance from those accustomed to traditional approaches.

1. Education and Training: Provide education and training on the benefits and principles of a restorative culture to help overcome resistance.

Do not conform to the pattern of this world, but be transformed by the renewing of your mind. (Romans 12:2)

2. Gradual Implementation: Introduce restorative practices gradually, allowing time for adjustment and acceptance.

Be patient, bearing with one another in love. (Ephesians 4:2)

Ensuring Fairness and Equity

Ensuring that restorative practices are applied fairly and equitably is essential for their success.

1. Inclusive Processes: Design inclusive processes that are accessible to all members, regardless of their background or status.

My brothers and sisters, believers in our glorious Lord Jesus Christ must not show favoritism. (James 2:1)

2. Regular Evaluation: Regularly evaluate restorative practices to ensure they are effective and fair, making adjustments as needed.

Test everything. Hold on to what is good, reject every kind of evil. (1 Thessalonians 5:21-22)

Fostering a culture of love and restoration within the church involves integrating the principles of love, forgiveness, and reconciliation into every aspect of church life. By teaching and modeling these values, building loving relationships, and implementing restorative practices, the church can create an environment that reflects the heart of the gospel.

Overcoming challenges and ensuring fairness and equity are essential for the success of these efforts, requiring ongoing commitment and leadership. By fostering a restorative mindset and encouraging community involvement, the church can build a culture that promotes healing, unity, and mutual support.

As we continue to draw lessons from Paul's writings, we can create a church that embodies the transformative power of love and restorative justice, reflecting God's redemptive work in all aspects of life.

CHAPTER 09

OVERCOMING BARRIERS TO RESTORATIVE JUSTICE

Restorative justice represents a transformative approach to dealing with harm and conflict, emphasizing healing, restoration, and reconciliation over punishment. However, implementing restorative justice practices within the church and broader community can be met with various challenges and obstacles. This chapter identifies common barriers to restorative justice and offers strategies for overcoming them, ensuring that these practices can be effectively integrated and sustained.

Common Challenges and Obstacles

Resistance to Change

One of the most significant barriers to implementing restorative justice is resistance to change. People often prefer familiar methods and may be skeptical of new approaches.

1. Traditional Mindsets: Many individuals and communities are accustomed to retributive justice, which focuses on punishment. Transitioning to restorative justice requires a shift in mindset.

You were taught, with regard to your former way of life, to put off your old self, which is being corrupted by its deceitful desires; to be made new in the attitude of your minds. (Ephesians 4:22-23)

2. Fear of the Unknown: People may fear the unknown and the potential for restorative practices to be perceived as too lenient or ineffective.

For God has not given us a spirit of fear and timidity but of power, love, and self-discipline. (2 Timothy 1:7)

Lack of Understanding and Awareness

Another significant barrier is a lack of understanding and awareness about restorative justice principles and practices.

1. Misinformation: There may be misconceptions about what restorative justice entails, leading to resistance and skepticism.

The heart of the discerning acquires knowledge, for the ears of the wise seek it out. (Proverbs 18:15)

2. Educational Gaps: Without proper education and training, individuals may not fully grasp the benefits and processes involved in restorative justice.

My people are destroyed by lack of knowledge. (Hosea 4:6)

Institutional and Systemic Barriers

Institutional and systemic barriers can also impede the implementation of restorative justice practices.

1. Rigid Structures: Established institutions and systems may have rigid structures and policies that are resistant to change.

When the sentence for a crime is not quickly carried out, people's hearts are filled with schemes to do wrong. (Ecclesiastes 8:11)

2. Resource Limitations: Implementing restorative justice practices requires resources, including trained facilitators, time, and funding, which may be limited.

Suppose one of you wants to build a tower. Won't you first sit down and estimate the cost to see if you have enough money to complete it? (Luke 14:28)

Cultural and Social Barriers

Cultural and social factors can also present significant challenges to restorative justice.

1. Cultural Norms: In some cultures, punitive approaches to justice are deeply ingrained, making restorative practices seem foreign or inappropriate.

Do not conform to the pattern of this world, but be transformed by the renewing of your mind. (Romans 12:2)

2. Social Stigmas: There may be social stigmas attached to offenders or victims that hinder the willingness to participate in restorative processes.

There is neither Jew nor Gentile, neither slave nor free, nor is there male and female, for you are all one in Christ Jesus. (Galatians 3:28)

Strategies for Overcoming Barriers

Education and Training

Providing comprehensive education and training is crucial for overcoming resistance and fostering an understanding of restorative justice.

1. Workshops and Seminars: Conduct workshops and seminars to educate church members and community leaders about the principles and benefits of restorative justice.

All Scripture is God-breathed and is useful for teaching, rebuking, correcting, and training in righteousness. (2 Timothy 3:16)

2. Ongoing Training: Offer ongoing training programs for facilitators, ensuring they are well-equipped to guide restorative processes.

The things you have heard me say in the presence of many witnesses entrust to reliable people who will also be qualified to teach others. (2 Timothy 2:2)

Building Support and Advocacy

Gaining support from key stakeholders and advocates can help overcome institutional and systemic barriers.

1. Engaging Leadership: Involve church and community leaders in the process, highlighting the alignment of restorative justice with biblical principles.

Remember your leaders, who spoke the word of God to you. Consider the outcome of their way of life and imitate their faith. (Hebrews 13:7)

2. Creating Advocacy Groups: Form advocacy groups within the church and community to champion restorative justice and promote its benefits.

Therefore encourage one another and build each other up, just as in fact you are doing. (1 Thessalonians 5:11)

Providing Resources and Support

Ensuring that adequate resources and support are available is essential for the successful implementation of restorative practices.

1. Funding and Resources: Seek funding and resources from various sources, including grants, donations, and community partnerships.

And my God will meet all your needs according to the riches of his glory in Christ Jesus. (Philippians 4:19)

2. Support Networks: Establish support networks for victims, offenders, and facilitators, providing the necessary emotional and practical support.

Carry each other's burdens, and in this way you will fulfill the law of Christ. (Galatians 6:2)

Cultivating a Restorative Culture

Creating a culture that values restorative justice requires intentional efforts to shift mindsets and practices.

1. Modeling Restorative Values: Leaders and influential members should model restorative values in their interactions and decision-making.

Follow my example, as I follow the example of Christ. (1 Corinthians 11:1)

2. Celebrating Successes: Highlight and celebrate successful restorative justice cases within the community, demonstrating their effectiveness.

Rejoice with those who rejoice; mourn with those who mourn. (Romans 12:15)

Practical Steps for Implementation

Integrating Restorative Practices

Integrate restorative practices into existing structures and processes within the church and community.

1. Restorative Policies: Develop and implement policies that incorporate restorative practices into the church's disciplinary and conflict resolution procedures.

But everything should be done in a fitting and orderly way. (1 Corinthians 14:40)

2. Inclusive Decision-Making: Involve various stakeholders in the decision-making process to ensure buy-in and commitment to restorative practices.

Plans fail for lack of counsel, but with many advisers they succeed. (Proverbs 15:22)

Monitoring and Evaluation

Regular monitoring and evaluation are crucial for assessing the effectiveness of restorative practices and making necessary adjustments.

1. Feedback Mechanisms: Implement feedback mechanisms to gather input from participants and stakeholders about their experiences with restorative justice.

Plans are established by seeking advice; so if you wage war, obtain guidance. (Proverbs 20:18)

2. Continuous Improvement: Use feedback and evaluation data to continuously improve restorative practices and address any emerging challenges.

Test everything. Hold on to what is good, reject every kind of evil. (1 Thessalonians 5:21-22)

Overcoming barriers to restorative justice requires a comprehensive and multifaceted approach, addressing resistance, lack of understanding, institutional constraints, and cultural challenges. By providing education and training, building support and advocacy, ensuring resources and support, and cultivating a restorative culture, the church and community can effectively integrate restorative practices.

Practical steps such as integrating restorative practices into existing structures, monitoring and evaluating their effectiveness, and celebrating successes can help sustain these efforts. By fostering a culture of love and restoration, the church can reflect the heart of the gospel, promoting healing, reconciliation, and justice in all aspects of community life.

As we continue to learn from Paul's teachings and apply these principles, we can create environments that embody the transformative power of restorative justice, contributing to the flourishing of individuals and communities alike.

ADDRESSING ISSUES OF POWER, PREJUDICE, AND RESISTANCE

Implementing restorative justice within the church and broader community often encounters significant challenges related to power dynamics, prejudice, and resistance. These issues can hinder the effective application of restorative practices and impede the pursuit of justice and reconciliation. This chapter explores strategies for addressing power imbalances, combating prejudice, and overcoming resistance to restorative justice, ensuring that these practices can be implemented equitably and effectively.

Understanding the Challenges

Power Dynamics

Power imbalances can significantly impact the implementation of restorative justice. Those in positions of authority may resist changes that challenge their control, while marginalized individuals may feel disempowered to participate fully.

1. Authority and Control: Individuals in positions of power may resist restorative practices that democratize decision-making and empower marginalized voices.

But many who are first will be last, and many who are last will be first. (Matthew 19:30)

2. Disempowerment of the Marginalized: Marginalized individuals may feel that their voices are not heard or valued within the existing power structures.

Speak up for those who cannot speak for themselves, for the rights of all who are destitute. (Proverbs 31:8)

Prejudice and Discrimination

Prejudice and discrimination can undermine the fairness and effectiveness of restorative justice practices, perpetuating inequalities and injustice.

1. Racial and Ethnic Prejudice: Racial and ethnic prejudices can influence how justice is administered, leading to biased outcomes.

There is neither Jew nor Gentile, neither slave nor free, nor is there male and female, for you are all one in Christ Jesus. (Galatians 3:28)

2. Gender and Socioeconomic Discrimination: Gender and socioeconomic discrimination can further marginalize vulnerable individuals, affecting their access to justice and support.

My brothers and sisters, believers in our glorious Lord Jesus Christ must not show favoritism. (James 2:1)

Resistance to Change

Resistance to change is a common barrier to implementing restorative justice. People may cling to familiar systems and fear the unknown aspects of new approaches.

1. Fear of the Unknown: Fear of the unknown and concerns about the effectiveness of restorative practices can lead to resistance.

For God has not given us a spirit of fear and timidity, but of power, love, and self-discipline. (2 Timothy 1:7)

2. Attachment to Traditional Practices: Attachment to traditional punitive practices can create a reluctance to adopt restorative methods.

Do not conform to the pattern of this world, but be transformed by the renewing of your mind. (Romans 12:2)

Strategies for Addressing Power Dynamics

Empowering Marginalized Voices

Creating spaces where marginalized individuals can speak and be heard is crucial for addressing power imbalances.

1. Inclusive Decision-Making: Ensure that marginalized voices are included in decision-making processes, giving them a platform to contribute.

Plans fail for lack of counsel, but with many advisers they succeed. (Proverbs 15:22)

2. Facilitating Dialogue: Use restorative circles and other dialogue methods to facilitate conversations where everyone has an equal opportunity to speak.

The way of fools seems right to them, but the wise listen to advice. (Proverbs 12:15)

Promoting Servant Leadership

Encouraging a model of servant leadership can help mitigate power imbalances and promote a culture of humility and service.

1. Leadership Training: Provide training for leaders on servant leadership principles, emphasizing humility, empathy, and service.

Not so with you. Instead, whoever wants to become great among you must be your servant. (Matthew 20:26)

2. Modeling Servant Leadership: Leaders should model servant leadership in their actions, demonstrating a commitment to serving others.

Follow my example, as I follow the example of Christ. (1 Corinthians 11:1)

Strategies for Combating Prejudice and Discrimination

Education and Awareness

Raising awareness and providing education about prejudice and discrimination can help combat these issues within the community.

1. Anti-Bias Training: Implement anti-bias training programs to help individuals recognize and address their own prejudices.

Do not judge, or you too will be judged. For in the same way you judge others, you will be judged, and with the measure you use, it will be measured to you. (Matthew 7:1-2)

2. Cultural Competency Workshops: Offer workshops on cultural competency to promote understanding and respect for diverse backgrounds.

Accept one another, then, just as Christ accepted you, in order to bring praise to God. (Romans 15:7)

Policy and Practice Reforms

Reforming policies and practices to ensure they are inclusive and equitable is essential for addressing systemic discrimination.

1. Equitable Policies: Develop and implement policies that promote equity and inclusivity, ensuring fair treatment for all individuals.

Learn to do right; seek justice. Defend the oppressed. Take up the cause of the fatherless; plead the case of the widow. (Isaiah 1:17)

2. Regular Review: Regularly review policies and practices to identify and address any discriminatory elements.

Test everything. Hold on to what is good, reject every kind of evil. (1 Thessalonians 5:21-22)

Strategies for Overcoming Resistance to Change

Building Understanding and Trust

Building understanding and trust is crucial for overcoming resistance and fostering acceptance of restorative practices.

1. Educational Initiatives: Provide comprehensive education on the principles and benefits of restorative justice, using evidence-based examples.

The heart of the discerning acquires knowledge, for the ears of the wise seek it out. (Proverbs 18:15)

2. Transparency and Communication: Maintain open and transparent communication about the implementation process and its outcomes, building trust and buy-in.

Speak the truth in love, and we will grow to become in every respect the mature body of him who is the head, that is, Christ. (Ephesians 4:15)

Gradual Implementation and Pilot Programs

Introducing restorative practices gradually can help alleviate fears and demonstrate their effectiveness.

1. Pilot Programs: Start with pilot programs to test restorative practices on a smaller scale, gather feedback, and make adjustments before wider implementation.

Suppose one of you wants to build a tower. Won't you first sit down and estimate the cost to see if you have enough money to complete it? (Luke 14:28)

2. Incremental Changes: Implement changes incrementally, allowing time for adjustment and acceptance.

Be patient, bearing with one another in love. (Ephesians 4:2)

Building a Supportive Culture

Promoting Restorative Values

Fostering a culture that values restorative justice requires promoting and modeling restorative values within the community.

1. Restorative Education: Integrate restorative justice principles into educational curricula and church teachings.

All Scripture is God-breathed and is useful for teaching, rebuking, correcting and training in righteousness. (2 Timothy 3:16)

2. Celebrating Successes: Highlight and celebrate successful restorative justice cases, demonstrating their positive impact on individuals and the community.

Rejoice with those who rejoice; mourn with those who mourn. (Romans 12:15)

Encouraging Community Involvement

Community involvement is key to the success of restorative practices, ensuring broad support and engagement.

1. Inclusive Processes: Ensure that restorative processes are inclusive, giving all community members a voice and a role.

Carry each other's burdens, and in this way you will fulfill the law of Christ. (Galatians 6:2)

2. Community Building Activities: Organize community-building activities that foster relationships and strengthen the sense of community.

Let us not give up meeting together, as some are in the habit of doing, but let us encourage one another—and all the more as you see the Day approaching. (Hebrews 10:25)

Addressing issues of power, prejudice, and resistance is essential for the successful implementation of restorative justice within the church and broader community. By empowering marginalized voices, promoting servant leadership, combating prejudice and discrimination, and overcoming resistance to change, communities can create environments where restorative practices can thrive.

Building understanding and trust, introducing changes gradually, and fostering a supportive culture are critical strategies for ensuring that restorative justice principles are integrated effectively. By drawing on Paul's teachings and biblical principles, the church can lead the way in promoting justice, reconciliation, and healing.

As we continue to apply these strategies and learn from our experiences, we can create communities that embody the transformative power of restorative justice, reflecting the heart of the gospel and promoting the flourishing of all individuals.

BUILDING TRUST AND FOSTERING OPEN COMMUNICATION

Trust and open communication are fundamental components of restorative justice. Without trust, individuals are unlikely to engage genuinely in restorative processes, and without open communication, misunderstandings and conflicts can escalate. This chapter explores strategies for building trust and fostering open communication within the church and the broader community to support the effective implementation of restorative justice practices.

The Importance of Trust in Restorative Justice

Trust as a Foundation

Trust is the bedrock upon which restorative justice is built. It enables participants to feel safe and supported, encouraging honest dialogue and genuine reconciliation.

1. Safety and Vulnerability: Trust creates a safe environment where individuals feel comfortable sharing their experiences and vulnerabilities.

There is no fear in love. But perfect love drives out fear because fear has to do with punishment. The one who fears is not made perfect in love. (1 John 4:18)

2. Building Relationships: Trust fosters strong relationships, essential for effective community building and conflict resolution.

A friend loves at all times, and a brother is born for a time of adversity. (Proverbs 17:17)

The Role of Trust in Healing

Trust is crucial for healing both individual and communal wounds. It allows for the acknowledgment of harm and the pursuit of forgiveness and reconciliation.

1. Acknowledgment of Harm: Trust enables victims to feel heard and acknowledged, which is a critical step in the healing process.

The Lord is close to the brokenhearted and saves those who are crushed in spirit. (Psalm 34:18)

2. Forgiveness and Reconciliation: Trust is essential for forgiveness and reconciliation, allowing both victims and offenders to move forward constructively.

Bear with each other and forgive one another if any of you has a grievance against someone. Forgive as the Lord forgave you. (Colossians 3:13)

Strategies for Building Trust

Consistent and Fair Practices

Consistency and fairness in the application of restorative practices help build trust within the community.

1. Transparency in Processes: Ensure that restorative justice processes are transparent, with clear guidelines and expectations.

But let justice roll on like a river, righteousness like a never-failing stream! (Amos 5:24)

2. Equitable Treatment: Apply restorative practices equitably, ensuring that all individuals are treated fairly and without bias.

Do not pervert justice; do not show partiality to the poor or favoritism to the great, but judge your neighbor fairly. (Leviticus 19:15)

Building Relationships and Community

Investing in relationship-building activities strengthens the sense of community and trust among members.

1. Small Groups and Fellowship: Encourage small groups and fellowship activities that promote deeper relationships and mutual support.

Let us consider how we may spur one another on toward love and good deeds, not giving up meeting together, as some are in the habit of doing but encouraging one another. (Hebrews 10:24-25)

2. Acts of Service: Engage in acts of service within the community, fostering a culture of care and support.

Each of you should use whatever gift you have received to serve others, as faithful stewards of God's grace in its various forms. (1 Peter 4:10)

Training and Education

Providing education and training on restorative practices helps build trust by demonstrating commitment and competence.

1. Restorative Justice Training: Offer comprehensive training on restorative justice principles and practices for church leaders and members.

The things you have heard me say in the presence of many witnesses entrust to reliable people who will also be qualified to teach others. (2 Timothy 2:2)

2. Ongoing Learning Opportunities: Provide ongoing learning opportunities to keep the community informed and engaged in restorative practices.

Grow in the grace and knowledge of our Lord and Savior Jesus Christ. To him be glory both now and forever! Amen. (2 Peter 3:18)

Fostering Open Communication

Creating Safe Spaces for Dialogue

Safe spaces for dialogue are essential for open communication, allowing individuals to express themselves without fear of judgment or retribution.

1. Restorative Circles: Use restorative circles to facilitate open dialogue, where all participants have an equal opportunity to speak and be heard.

Therefore, if you are offering your gift at the altar and there remember that your brother or sister has something against you, leave your gift there in front of the altar. First, go and be reconciled to them; then come and offer your gift. (Matthew 5:23-24)

2. Confidentiality and Respect: Ensure that all conversations within restorative processes are confidential and conducted with respect.

Do not let any unwholesome talk come out of your mouths, but only what is helpful for building others up according to their needs, that it may benefit those who listen. (Ephesians 4:29)

Encouraging Active Listening

Active listening is crucial for effective communication, ensuring that all voices are heard and understood.

1. Training in Active Listening: Provide training on active listening skills, emphasizing empathy and understanding.

Everyone should be quick to listen, slow to speak, and slow to become angry. (James 1:19)

2. Modeling Active Listening: Leaders and facilitators should model active listening in all interactions, setting a positive example for others.

My dear brothers and sisters, take note of this: Everyone should be quick to listen, slow to speak and slow to become angry. (James 1:19)

Promoting Honest and Open Dialogue

Encouraging honesty and openness in communication helps build trust and address conflicts constructively.

1. Honest Communication: Encourage honest and open communication, where individuals feel free to express their thoughts and feelings.

Therefore each of you must put off falsehood and speak truthfully to your neighbor, for we are all members of one body. (Ephesians 4:25)

2. Conflict Resolution Skills: Provide training in conflict resolution skills, helping individuals address issues constructively and peacefully.

If your brother or sister sins, go and point out their fault, just between the two of you. If they listen to you, you have won them over. (Matthew 18:15)

Overcoming Barriers to Trust and Communication

Addressing Mistrust and Suspicion

Mistrust and suspicion can be significant barriers to effective communication and restorative practices.

1. Building Trust Over Time: Trust is built over time through consistent and fair actions. Be patient and persistent in efforts to build trust.

Let us not become weary in doing good, for at the proper time we will reap a harvest if we do not give up. (Galatians 6:9)

2. Transparency and Accountability: Maintain transparency and accountability in all actions and decisions to build credibility and trust.

But you, Timothy, are a man of God; so run from all these evil things. Pursue righteousness and a godly life, along with faith, love, perseverance, and gentleness. (1 Timothy 6:11)

Navigating Cultural and Social Barriers

Cultural and social differences can create communication barriers that need to be addressed proactively.

1. Cultural Competency: Provide training on cultural competency to promote understanding and respect for diverse backgrounds.

Accept one another, then, just as Christ accepted you, in order to bring praise to God. (Romans 15:7)

2. Inclusive Practices: Implement inclusive practices that ensure all voices are heard and valued, regardless of cultural or social background.

There is neither Jew nor Gentile, neither slave nor free, nor is there male and female, for you are all one in Christ Jesus. (Galatians 3:28)

Building a Supportive Community

Encouraging Community Involvement

Community involvement is crucial for fostering trust and open communication within restorative practices.

1.   Collaborative   Decision-Making: Involve community members in decision-making processes, ensuring that everyone has a voice.

Plans fail for lack of counsel, but with many advisers, they succeed. (Proverbs 15:22)

2. Community Building Activities: Organize activities that build relationships and strengthen the sense of community.

Let us consider how we may spur one another on toward love and good deeds, not giving up meeting together, as some are in the habit of doing but encouraging one another. (Hebrews 10:24-25)

Providing Support Networks

Support networks provide the necessary resources and encouragement for individuals to engage in restorative practices.

1. Peer Support Groups: Establish peer support groups where individuals can share their experiences and support one another.

Carry each other's burdens, and in this way you will fulfill the law of Christ. (Galatians 6:2)

2. Mentorship Programs: Implement mentorship programs where more experienced individuals can guide and support those new to restorative practices.

Follow my example, as I follow the example of Christ. (1 Corinthians 11:1)

Building trust and fostering open communication is essential for the successful implementation of restorative justice practices within the church and broader community. By creating safe spaces for dialogue, encouraging active listening, promoting honest communication, and addressing barriers to trust, communities can create environments where restorative practices can thrive.

Investing in relationship-building activities, providing education and training, and ensuring transparency and accountability are critical strategies for building trust. Fostering open communication through inclusive and respectful dialogue helps

STRATEGIES FOR SUCCESSFUL IMPLEMENTATION OF RESTORATIVE JUSTICE

Implementing restorative justice within the church and broader community requires careful planning, commitment, and strategic action. Successful implementation involves addressing practical, cultural, and systemic challenges while fostering an environment of trust, respect, and openness. This chapter outlines strategies for effectively introducing and sustaining restorative justice practices, ensuring they are deeply embedded and widely supported.

Developing a Clear Vision and Mission

Articulating the Vision

A clear and compelling vision for restorative justice provides direction and motivation for the community.

1. Defining Goals: Clearly define the goals and desired outcomes of restorative justice practices within the community.

Where there is no vision, the people perish. (Proverbs 29:18)

2. Aligning with Biblical Principles: Ensure that the vision aligns with biblical principles of justice, mercy, and reconciliation.

He has shown you, O mortal, what is good. And what does the Lord require of you? To act justly and to love mercy and to walk humbly with your God. (Micah 6:8)

Creating a Mission Statement

A mission statement succinctly communicates the purpose and scope of restorative justice initiatives.

1. Inclusive Language: Use inclusive and inspiring language that resonates with the entire community.

Make every effort to keep the unity of the Spirit through the bond of peace. (Ephesians 4:3)

2. Action-Oriented: Highlight specific actions and commitments that the community will undertake.

Whatever you do, work at it with all your heart, as working for the Lord, not for human masters. (Colossians 3:23)

Building a Strong Foundation

Securing Leadership Support

Strong leadership support is crucial for the successful implementation of restorative justice practices.

1. Engaging Leaders: Involve church and community leaders in the planning and implementation process.

Remember your leaders, who spoke the word of God to you. Consider the outcome of their way of life and imitate their faith. (Hebrews 13:7)

2. Leadership Training: Provide training for leaders on restorative justice principles and practices.

The things you have heard me say in the presence of many witnesses entrust to reliable people who will also be qualified to teach others. (2 Timothy 2:2)

Establishing a Coordinating Team

A dedicated team to coordinate restorative justice efforts ensures focused and consistent implementation.

1. Diverse Representation: Ensure the team includes diverse members representing different segments of the community.

For just as each of us has one body with many members, and these members do not all have the same function, so in Christ we, though many, form one body, and each member belongs to all the others. (Romans 12:4-5)

2. Clear Roles and Responsibilities: Define clear roles and responsibilities for team members to ensure accountability and efficiency.

And whatever you do, whether in word or deed, do it all in the name of the Lord Jesus, giving thanks to God the Father through him. (Colossians 3:17)

Engaging the Community

Education and Training

Comprehensive education and training are essential for fostering understanding and support for restorative justice.

1. Workshops and Seminars: Organize workshops and seminars to educate community members about restorative justice principles and benefits.

Let the wise listen and add to their learning, and let the discerning get guidance. (Proverbs 1:5)

2. Ongoing Training Programs: Provide ongoing training programs to keep the community informed and engaged.

Grow in the grace and knowledge of our Lord and Savior Jesus Christ. To him be glory both now and forever! Amen. (2 Peter 3:18)

Raising Awareness

Raising awareness about restorative justice helps build broad-based support and understanding.

1. Communication Campaigns: Use various communication channels, including social media, newsletters, and community meetings, to raise awareness.

So whether you eat or drink or whatever you do, do it all for the glory of God. (1 Corinthians 10:31)

2. Success Stories: Share success stories and testimonials to demonstrate the positive impact of restorative justice practices.

They triumphed over him by the blood of the Lamb and by the word of their testimony. (Revelation 12:11)

Implementing Restorative Practices

Establishing Restorative Processes

Clearly defined restorative processes are critical for consistent and effective practice.

1. Restorative Circles: Implement restorative circles as a primary method for addressing conflicts and harms.

Therefore, if you are offering your gift at the altar and there remember that your brother or sister has something against you, leave your gift there in front of the altar. First, go and be reconciled to them; then come and offer your gift. (Matthew 5:23-24)

2. Mediation and Facilitation: Train mediators and facilitators to guide restorative processes and ensure they are conducted fairly and effectively.

Blessed are the peacemakers, for they will be called children of God. (Matthew 5:9)

Providing Support and Resources

Adequate support and resources are essential for sustaining restorative justice initiatives.

1. Funding and Resources: Seek funding and resources from various sources, including grants, donations, and partnerships.

And my God will meet all your needs according to the riches of his glory in Christ Jesus. (Philippians 4:19)

2. Support Networks: Establish support networks for victims, offenders, and facilitators to provide the necessary emotional and practical support.

Carry each other's burdens, and in this way you will fulfill the law of Christ. (Galatians 6:2)

Monitoring and Evaluation

Regular Monitoring

Regular monitoring helps ensure that restorative practices are being implemented effectively and equitably.

1. Feedback Mechanisms: Implement feedback mechanisms to gather input from participants and stakeholders about their experiences.

Plans are established by seeking advice; so if you wage war, obtain guidance. (Proverbs 20:18)

2. Data Collection: Collect data on the outcomes of restorative processes to assess their impact and effectiveness.

Examine yourselves to see whether you are in the faith; test yourselves. Do you not realize that Christ Jesus is in you—unless, of course, you fail the test? (2 Corinthians 13:5)

Continuous Improvement

Continuous improvement ensures that restorative practices remain relevant and effective.

1. Regular Review: Regularly review and assess restorative practices to identify areas for improvement.

Test everything. Hold on to what is good, reject every kind of evil. (1 Thessalonians 5:21-22)

2. Adapting to Feedback: Use feedback and evaluation data to make necessary adjustments and improvements.

Listen to advice and accept discipline, and at the end you will be counted among the wise. (Proverbs 19:20)

Fostering a Culture of Restorative Justice

Promoting Restorative Values

Embedding restorative values into the community culture ensures long-term sustainability and acceptance.

1. Restorative Education: Integrate restorative justice principles into educational curricula and church teachings.

All Scripture is God-breathed and is useful for teaching, rebuking, correcting and training in righteousness. (2 Timothy 3:16)

2. Role Modeling: Leaders and influential members should model restorative values in their actions and decisions.

Follow my example, as I follow the example of Christ. (1 Corinthians 11:1)

Encouraging Community Involvement

Broad-based community involvement is key to the success of restorative justice initiatives.

1. Inclusive Processes: Ensure that restorative processes are inclusive, giving all community members a voice and a role.

Let each of you look not only to his own interests but also to the interests of others. (Philippians 2:4)

2. Community Building Activities: Organize activities that build relationships and strengthen the sense of community.

Let us consider how we may spur one another on toward love and good deeds, not giving up meeting together, as some are in the habit of doing but encouraging one another. (Hebrews 10:24-25)

Successful implementation of restorative justice within the church and broader community requires a strategic and comprehensive approach. Developing a clear vision and mission, building a strong foundation, engaging the community, implementing effective restorative practices, and fostering a culture of restorative justice are essential steps.

By securing leadership support, providing education and training, raising awareness, and ensuring consistent and fair practices, communities can create environments where restorative justice thrives. Regular monitoring and continuous improvement help sustain these efforts, ensuring they remain effective and relevant.

As we continue to apply these strategies and learn from our experiences, we can build communities that embody the transformative power of restorative justice, reflecting the heart of the gospel and promoting healing, reconciliation, and justice for all.

CHAPTER 10

CONTEMPORARY APPLICATIONS OF PAUL'S TEACHINGS

Restorative Justice in Modern Church Settings

The teachings of the Apostle Paul provide a profound foundation for restorative justice, emphasizing love, forgiveness, and reconciliation. These principles are timeless and offer valuable guidance for addressing conflict and harm in modern church settings. This chapter explores how Paul's teachings can be applied to contemporary church environments to foster restorative justice, heal broken relationships, and build stronger, more compassionate communities.

Understanding Paul's Teachings on Restorative Justice

Love and Forgiveness

Paul consistently emphasizes love and forgiveness as central to Christian life and community.

1. The Centrality of Love: Paul's teaching in 1 Corinthians 13 highlights that love is the greatest virtue and the foundation of all Christian behavior.

And now these three remain faith, hope, and love. But the greatest of these is love. (1 Corinthians 13:13)

2. The Necessity of Forgiveness: Forgiveness is essential for healing and reconciliation, as Paul teaches in Colossians 3:13.

Bear with each other and forgive one another if any of you has a grievance against someone. Forgive as the Lord forgave you. (Colossians 3:13)

Reconciliation and Unity

Paul's writings emphasize the importance of reconciliation and unity within the Christian community.

1. The Ministry of Reconciliation: In 2 Corinthians 5:18-19, Paul describes the ministry of reconciliation given to believers.

All this is from God, who reconciled us to himself through Christ and gave us the ministry of reconciliation: that God was reconciling the world to himself in Christ, not counting people's sins against them. (2 Corinthians 5:18-19)

2. Unity in Christ: Paul teaches that all believers are united in Christ, breaking down social and cultural barriers.

There is neither Jew nor Gentile, neither slave nor free, nor is there male and female, for you are all one in Christ Jesus. (Galatians 3:28)

Applying Paul's Teachings in Modern Church Settings

Establishing Restorative Practices

Integrating restorative practices into church life helps address conflicts and harms constructively.

1. Restorative Circles: Use restorative circles to address conflicts, allowing all parties to share their perspectives and work towards resolution.

Therefore, if you are offering your gift at the altar and remember that your brother or sister has something against you, leave your gift there in front of the altar. First, go and be reconciled to them; then come and offer your gift. (Matthew 5:23-24)

2. Mediation and Facilitation: Train church members to serve as mediators and facilitators in restorative processes.

Blessed are the peacemakers, for they will be called children of God. (Matthew 5:9)

Promoting a Culture of Forgiveness

Fostering a culture of forgiveness helps create an environment where healing and reconciliation can flourish.

1. Teaching and Preaching on Forgiveness: Regularly teach and preach about the importance of forgiveness, using biblical examples and practical applications.

Bear with each other and forgive one another if any of you has a grievance against someone. Forgive as the Lord forgave you. (Colossians 3:13)

2. Encouraging Personal Reflection: Encourage members to reflect on their own need for forgiveness and their capacity to forgive others.

Forgive us our debts, as we also have forgiven our debtors. (Matthew 6:12)

Building Inclusive and Supportive Communities

Creating inclusive and supportive communities is essential for effective restorative justice.

1. Small Groups and Fellowship: Promote small groups and fellowship activities that foster deep, supportive relationships.

Let us consider how we may spur one another on toward love and good deeds, not giving up meeting together, as some are in the habit of doing but encouraging one another. (Hebrews 10:24-25)

2. Acts of Service: Encourage acts of service within the church and broader community, building a culture of care and support.

Each of you should use whatever gift you have received to serve others, as faithful stewards of God's grace in its various forms. (1 Peter 4:10)

Addressing Challenges and Obstacles

Overcoming Resistance to Change

Resistance to change can be a significant barrier to implementing restorative justice practices.

1. Education and Training: Provide education and training on the benefits and principles of restorative justice to help overcome resistance.

Do not conform to the pattern of this world, but be transformed by the renewing of your mind. (Romans 12:2)

2. Leadership Support: Engage church leaders in the process to gain their support and endorsement.

Remember your leaders, who spoke the word of God to you. Consider the outcome of their way of life and imitate their faith. (Hebrews 13:7)

Addressing Power Dynamics

Power imbalances can hinder the fair and effective implementation of restorative justice.

1. Empowering Marginalized Voices: Create opportunities for marginalized voices to be heard and valued.

Speak up for those who cannot speak for themselves, for the rights of all who are destitute. (Proverbs 31:8)

2. Promoting Servant Leadership: Encourage a model of servant leadership that prioritizes humility and service.

Not so with you. Instead, whoever wants to become great among you must be your servant. (Matthew 20:26)

Practical Steps for Implementation

Developing Restorative Policies

Developing clear policies for restorative justice helps ensure consistency and fairness.

1. Restorative Justice Framework: Develop a framework that outlines the principles and processes of restorative justice within the church.

But everything should be done in a fitting and orderly way. (1 Corinthians 14:40)

2. Inclusive Decision-Making: Involve diverse community members in developing these policies to ensure they are inclusive and representative.

Plans fail for lack of counsel, but with many advisers, they succeed. (Proverbs 15:22)

Providing Resources and Support

Adequate resources and support are essential for sustaining restorative justice initiatives.

1. Funding and Resources: Seek funding and resources from various sources, including grants, donations, and partnerships.

And my God will meet all your needs according to the riches of his glory in Christ Jesus. (Philippians 4:19)

2. Support Networks: Establish support networks for victims, offenders, and facilitators to provide the necessary emotional and practical support.

Carry each other's burdens, and in this way you will fulfill the law of Christ. (Galatians 6:2)

Fostering a Culture of Restorative Justice

Promoting Restorative Values

Embedding restorative values into the church culture ensures long-term sustainability and acceptance.

1. Restorative Education: Integrate restorative justice principles into educational curricula and church teachings.

All Scripture is God-breathed and is useful for teaching, rebuking, correcting, and training in righteousness. (2 Timothy 3:16)

2. Role Modeling: Leaders and influential members should model restorative values in their actions and decisions.

Follow my example, as I follow the example of Christ. (1 Corinthians 11:1)

Encouraging Community Involvement

Broad-based community involvement is key to the success of restorative justice initiatives.

1. Inclusive Processes: Ensure that restorative processes are inclusive, giving all community members a voice and a role.

Let each of you look not only to his own interests but also to the interests of others. (Philippians 2:4)

2. Community Building Activities: Organize activities that build relationships and strengthen the sense of community.

Let us consider how we may spur one another on toward love and good deeds, not giving up meeting together, as some are in the habit of doing but encouraging one another. (Hebrews 10:24-25)

Applying Paul's teachings on restorative justice in modern church settings involves a comprehensive approach that integrates love, forgiveness, and reconciliation into every aspect of church life. By establishing restorative practices, promoting a culture of forgiveness, building inclusive and supportive communities, and addressing challenges and obstacles, the church can create an environment where restorative justice thrives.

Developing clear policies, providing resources and support, and fostering a culture of restorative justice through education and community involvement are critical steps for successful implementation. As we continue to learn from Paul's teachings and apply these principles, we can build communities that embody the transformative power of restorative justice, reflecting the heart of the gospel and promoting healing, reconciliation, and justice for all.

CASE STUDIES AND REAL-LIFE EXAMPLES

The principles of restorative justice, as taught by Apostle Paul, have been successfully applied in various modern church settings and communities. This chapter presents several case studies and real-life examples that demonstrate the transformative power of restorative justice. These stories illustrate how churches and communities have implemented restorative practices to heal relationships, restore trust, and promote reconciliation.

Case Study 1: Reconciliation in a Local Church

Background

A local church in the Midwest faced a significant conflict between two long-standing members, John and

Sarah. The disagreement, initially about church management decisions, escalated to personal attacks and division within the congregation.

Implementation of Restorative Practices

1. Restorative Circles: The church leadership introduced restorative circles to address the conflict. Both John and Sarah, along with affected church members, participated in facilitated circles to discuss their grievances and feelings.

Therefore, if you are offering your gift at the altar and there remember that your brother or sister has something against you, leave your gift there in front of the altar. First, go and be reconciled to them; then come and offer your gift. (Matthew 5:23-24)

2. Mediation: Trained mediators from the church facilitated private sessions between John and Sarah, helping them to understand each other's perspectives and work towards reconciliation.

Blessed are the peacemakers, for they will be called children of God. (Matthew 5:9)

Outcomes

- Healing and Forgiveness: Through the restorative processes, John and Sarah were able to express their feelings, acknowledge the harm caused, and forgive each other.

- Restored Relationships: The church community witnessed the restoration of relationships, resulting in a more united and supportive congregation.

- Continued Commitment: The church is committed to ongoing training and implementation of restorative practices, fostering a culture of forgiveness and reconciliation.

Case Study 2: Restorative Justice in Youth Ministry

Background

A youth ministry in a large urban church experienced a severe incident involving bullying. Several teenagers were affected, leading to a fractured and hostile environment.

Implementation of Restorative Practices

1. Restorative Justice Workshops: The church organized workshops to educate the youth and their parents about restorative justice principles.

Train up a child in the way he should go; even when he is old he will not depart from it. (Proverbs 22:6)

2. Restorative Circles: Facilitated circles were conducted, allowing the victims and the perpetrators to share their experiences and feelings in a safe environment.

Fathers, do not provoke your children to anger, but bring them up in the discipline and instruction of the Lord. (Ephesians 6:4)

3. Peer Mediation: Selected youth were trained as peer mediators to help resolve future conflicts, promoting a sense of responsibility and empowerment among teenagers.

Let no one despise your youth, but set the believers an example in speech, in conduct, in love, in faith, in purity. (1 Timothy 4:12)

Outcomes

- Improved Relationships: The bullying incidents decreased significantly, and relationships among the youth improved.

- Empowered Youth: The peer mediation program empowered the youth to take active roles in conflict resolution, fostering leadership and accountability.

- Positive Environment: The youth ministry became a more positive and supportive environment, encouraging open communication and mutual respect.

Case Study 3: Community-Wide Restorative Justice Initiative

Background

A community plagued by high crime rates and distrust between residents and law enforcement sought to implement restorative justice to address these issues.

Implementation of Restorative Practices

1. Community Dialogues: The local church partnered with community organizations to host dialogues between residents and law enforcement officials.

Love your neighbor as yourself. (Matthew 22:39)

2. Restorative Justice Circles: Restorative justice circles were introduced to address specific incidents of crime and conflict, involving victims, offenders, and community members.

Do not be overcome by evil, but overcome evil with good. (Romans 12:21)

3. Reintegration Programs: Programs were developed to help reintegrate offenders into the community, providing them with support and opportunities for making amends.

If anyone is caught in a sin, you who live by the Spirit should restore that person gently. (Galatians 6:1)

Outcomes

- Restored Trust: The dialogues and circles helped restore trust between the community and law enforcement, leading to better cooperation and understanding.

- Reduced Crime Rates: Crime rates in the community decreased as restorative practices addressed underlying issues and promoted healing.

- Community Cohesion: The community became more cohesive, with residents actively participating in creating a safer and more supportive environment.

Case Study 4: Restorative Justice in a Multicultural Church

Background

A multicultural church in a diverse neighborhood faced cultural tensions and misunderstandings among its members, affecting the church's unity and mission.

Implementation of Restorative Practices

1. Cultural Competency Training: The church provided cultural competency training to educate members about different cultures and promote mutual respect.

Accept one another, then, just as Christ accepted you, in order to bring praise to God. (Romans 15:7)

2. Restorative Circles: Circles were used to address specific conflicts and misunderstandings, allowing members to share their cultural perspectives and experiences.

There is neither Jew nor Gentile, neither slave nor free, nor is there male and female, for you are all one in Christ Jesus. (Galatians 3:28)

3. Inclusive Worship Services: Worship services were designed to be inclusive, incorporating elements from various cultures represented in the congregation.

How good and pleasant it is when God's people live together in unity! (Psalm 133:1)

Outcomes

- Enhanced Understanding: Members gained a better understanding of each other's cultures, reducing tensions and fostering respect.

- Strengthened Unity: The church experienced strengthened unity and a deeper sense of community.

- Broadened Mission: The inclusive approach enhanced the church's mission and outreach, attracting a more diverse congregation.

These case studies and real-life examples illustrate the transformative impact of applying Paul's teachings on restorative justice in modern church settings. By implementing restorative practices such as restorative circles, mediation, cultural competency training, and community dialogues, churches and communities can address conflicts, heal relationships, and build stronger, more cohesive environments.

The success of these initiatives highlights the importance of education, leadership support, and community involvement in fostering a culture of restorative justice. As churches continue to draw on Paul's teachings and integrate these principles into their practices, they can promote healing, reconciliation, and justice, reflecting the heart of the gospel and contributing to the flourishing of individuals and communities.

INTEGRATING RESTORATIVE PRACTICES IN VARIOUS MINISTRIES

Integrating restorative justice practices into various church ministries can significantly enhance their effectiveness and foster a culture of healing, reconciliation, and justice. This chapter explores practical strategies for incorporating restorative practices into different ministries, including youth ministry, adult education, pastoral care, and community outreach.

Youth Ministry

Building a Foundation of Respect and Empathy

Youth ministry is an ideal setting for introducing restorative practices, as it helps young people develop respect and empathy.

1. Restorative Justice Education: Incorporate lessons on restorative justice into the youth curriculum, emphasizing the importance of empathy, forgiveness, and reconciliation.

Train up a child in the way he should go; even when he is old he will not depart from it. (Proverbs 22:6)

2. Role-Playing Exercises: Use role-playing exercises to help youth practice restorative conversations and understand different perspectives.

Let no one despise your youth, but set the believers an example in speech, in conduct, in love, in faith, in purity. (1 Timothy 4:12)

Addressing Conflict and Bullying

Restorative practices can effectively address issues like conflict and bullying within youth groups.

1. Restorative Circles: Implement restorative circles to address incidents of conflict or bullying, allowing all parties to express their feelings and work towards resolution.

If your brother or sister sins, go and point out their fault, just between the two of you. If they listen to you, you have won them over. (Matthew 18:15)

2. Peer Mediation Programs: Train youth as peer mediators to help resolve conflicts among their peers, fostering a sense of responsibility and leadership.

Blessed are the peacemakers, for they will be called children of God. (Matthew 5:9)

Adult Education

Fostering a Culture of Lifelong Learning

Adult education programs can integrate restorative practices to promote lifelong learning and personal growth.

1. Workshops and Seminars: Offer workshops and seminars on restorative justice, exploring its principles and applications in everyday life.

The heart of the discerning acquires knowledge, for the ears of the wise seek it out. (Proverbs 18:15)

2. Study Groups: Form study groups focused on restorative justice, encouraging participants to delve deeper into biblical and contemporary texts on the subject.

Let the wise listen and add to their learning, and let the discerning get guidance. (Proverbs 1:5)

Addressing Adult Conflicts

Restorative practices can help address conflicts among adults, promoting reconciliation and unity.

1. Mediation Sessions: Facilitate mediation sessions to resolve conflicts, with trained mediators guiding the process.

Bear with each other and forgive one another if any of you has a grievance against someone. Forgive as the Lord forgave you. (Colossians 3:13)

2. Restorative Conversations: Encourage restorative conversations where individuals can openly discuss their issues and seek mutual understanding.

Therefore each of you must put off falsehood and speak truthfully to your neighbor, for we are all members of one body. (Ephesians 4:25)

Pastoral Care

Providing Emotional and Spiritual Support

Restorative practices can enhance pastoral care by providing emotional and spiritual support to those in need.

1. Healing Circles: Use healing circles to support individuals dealing with grief, trauma, or other emotional challenges, creating a safe space for sharing and healing.

The Lord is close to the brokenhearted and saves those who are crushed in spirit. (Psalm 34:18)

2. One-on-One Counseling: Incorporate restorative principles into one-on-one counseling sessions, focusing on empathy, active listening, and reconciliation.

Carry each other's burdens, and in this way you will fulfill the law of Christ. (Galatians 6:2)

Addressing Congregational Conflicts

Pastoral care can also involve addressing conflicts within the congregation, and promoting peace and unity.

1. Conflict Resolution Training: Provide conflict resolution training for pastoral staff, equipping them with the skills to handle disputes effectively.

Peacemakers who sow in peace reap a harvest of righteousness. (James 3:18)

2. Restorative Processes: Implement restorative processes to address congregational conflicts, ensuring that all voices are heard and that solutions are fair and just.

If it is possible, as far as it depends on you, live at peace with everyone. (Romans 12:18)

Community Outreach

Building Stronger Community Relationships

Restorative practices can be a powerful tool in community outreach, helping to build stronger, more resilient communities.

1. Community Dialogues: Organize community dialogues that bring together diverse groups to discuss common issues and work towards collective solutions.

How good and pleasant it is when God's people live together in unity! (Psalm 133:1)

2. Restorative Justice Programs: Partner with local organizations to implement restorative justice programs that address crime and conflict within the community.

Do not be overcome by evil, but overcome evil with good. (Romans 12:21)

Supporting Vulnerable Populations

Restorative practices can also support vulnerable populations, providing them with the resources and support they need.

1. Reintegration Programs: Develop reintegration programs for formerly incarcerated individuals, helping them to rebuild their lives and reintegrate into the community.

If anyone is caught in a sin, you who live by the Spirit should restore that person gently. (Galatians 6:1)

2. Support Groups: Establish support groups for victims of crime, abuse, or other forms of trauma, providing a safe space for healing and recovery.

The Lord is a refuge for the oppressed, a stronghold in times of trouble. (Psalm 9:9)

Integrating Restorative Practices Across Ministries

Creating a Cohesive Approach

Integrating restorative practices across various ministries requires a cohesive approach that ensures consistency and support.

1. Unified Vision and Mission: Develop a unified vision and mission for restorative justice that encompasses all ministries within the church.

Where there is no vision, the people perish. (Proverbs 29:18)

2. Collaborative Efforts: Encourage collaboration between different ministries to share resources, ideas, and support.

For just as each of us has one body with many members, and these members do not all have the same function, so in Christ we, though many, form one body, and each member belongs to all the others. (Romans 12:4-5)

Providing Continuous Training and Support

Continuous training and support are essential for sustaining restorative practices across ministries.

1. Ongoing Education: Provide ongoing education and training opportunities for ministry leaders and volunteers to keep them informed and engaged.

The heart of the discerning acquires knowledge, for the ears of the wise seek it out. (Proverbs 18:15)

2. Resource Sharing: Create a central repository of resources, including training materials, guides, and case studies, accessible to all ministries.

Therefore encourage one another and build each other up, just as in fact you are doing. (1 Thessalonians 5:11)

Integrating restorative practices into various ministries can significantly enhance their effectiveness and contribute to a culture of healing, reconciliation, and justice within the church. By incorporating restorative principles into youth ministry, adult education, pastoral care, and community outreach, churches can address conflicts, support vulnerable individuals, and build stronger, more cohesive communities.

Creating a cohesive approach, providing continuous training and support, and fostering collaboration across ministries are essential for successful integration. As churches continue to draw on Paul's teachings and apply these principles, they can promote healing, reconciliation, and justice, reflecting the heart of the gospel and contributing to the flourishing of individuals and communities.

THE FUTURE OF RESTORATIVE JUSTICE IN CHRISTIAN COMMUNITIES

Restorative justice, deeply rooted in biblical principles, has the potential to transform Christian communities by fostering healing, reconciliation, and justice. As churches continue to embrace these practices, the future of restorative justice within Christian settings holds great promise. This chapter explores emerging trends, potential challenges, and strategies for advancing restorative justice in Christian communities, ensuring it remains a vital and transformative part of church life.

Emerging Trends in Restorative Justice

Increased Awareness and Education

Awareness and education about restorative justice are growing, with more churches recognizing its value and integrating its principles.

1. Educational Programs: Churches are increasingly offering educational programs and workshops to teach members about restorative justice.

The heart of the discerning acquires knowledge, for the ears of the wise seek it out. (Proverbs 18:15)

2. Theological Education: Seminaries and theological institutions are incorporating restorative justice into their curricula, preparing future leaders to champion these practices.

Train up a child in the way he should go; even when he is old he will not depart from it. (Proverbs 22:6)

Technology and Restorative Justice

Technology is playing a significant role in advancing restorative justice, providing new tools and platforms for education and implementation.

1. Online Training: Online training programs and webinars make restorative justice education more accessible to a broader audience.

So whether you eat or drink or whatever you do, do it all for the glory of God. (1 Corinthians 10:31)

2. Digital Platforms: Digital platforms facilitate restorative justice practices, such as virtual restorative circles and online mediation sessions.

The lips of the wise spread knowledge; not so the hearts of fools. (Proverbs 15:7)

Collaborative Networks

Collaborative networks and partnerships are essential for the growth and sustainability of restorative justice practices.

1. Inter-Church Collaboration: Churches are forming networks to share resources, best practices, and support for restorative justice initiatives.

How good and pleasant it is when God's people live together in unity! (Psalm 133:1)

2. Community Partnerships: Collaborations with community organizations, schools, and local governments enhance the impact of restorative justice programs.

Two are better than one, because they have a good return for their labor. (Ecclesiastes 4:9)

Potential Challenges and Solutions

Resistance to Change

Resistance to change remains a significant challenge for the widespread adoption of restorative justice practices.

1. Addressing Skepticism: Education and awareness campaigns can address skepticism by demonstrating the effectiveness and biblical foundation of restorative justice.

Do not conform to the pattern of this world, but be transformed by the renewing of your mind. (Romans 12:2)

2. Leadership Endorsement: Gaining support from church leaders is crucial for overcoming resistance and encouraging acceptance.

Remember your leaders, who spoke the word of God to you. Consider the outcome of their way of life and imitate their faith. (Hebrews 13:7)

Ensuring Fairness and Equity

Ensuring fairness and equity in restorative justice practices is essential for their credibility and success.

1. Inclusive Practices: Implement inclusive practices that ensure all voices are heard and respected, regardless of background or status.

My brothers and sisters, believers in our glorious Lord Jesus Christ must not show favoritism. (James 2:1)

2. Regular Evaluation: Regularly evaluate restorative justice programs to identify and address any biases or inequities.

Test everything. Hold on to what is good, reject every kind of evil. (1 Thessalonians 5:21-22)

Resource Limitations

Resource limitations can hinder the implementation and sustainability of restorative justice programs.

1. Securing Funding: Seek funding from various sources, including grants, donations, and partnerships, to support restorative justice initiatives.

And my God will meet all your needs according to the riches of his glory in Christ Jesus. (Philippians 4:19)

2. Volunteers and Training: Recruit and train volunteers to assist with restorative justice practices, providing the necessary support and resources.

Whatever you do, work at it with all your heart, as working for the Lord, not for human masters. (Colossians 3:23)

Strategies for Advancing Restorative Justice

Strengthening Theological Foundations

Strengthening the theological foundations of restorative justice can enhance its acceptance and integration within Christian communities.

1. Biblical Teaching: Emphasize the biblical basis for restorative justice in sermons, Bible studies, and educational programs.

He has shown you, O mortal, what is good. And what does the Lord require of you? To act justly and to love mercy and to walk humbly with your God. (Micah 6:8)

2. Theological Research: Encourage theological research and writing on restorative justice to deepen understanding and provide robust theological support.

But grow in the grace and knowledge of our Lord and Savior Jesus Christ. To him be glory both now and forever! Amen. (2 Peter 3:18)

Expanding Restorative Practices

Expanding restorative practices across different ministries and community settings can increase their impact and sustainability.

1. Integrating into Ministries: Integrate restorative justice practices into various church ministries, such as youth groups, adult education, and pastoral care.

For just as each of us has one body with many members, and these members do not all have the same function, so in Christ we, though many, form one body, and each member belongs to all the others. (Romans 12:4-5)

2. Community Outreach: Extend restorative justice practices beyond the church to address community conflicts and support vulnerable populations.

Do not be overcome by evil, but overcome evil with good. (Romans 12:21)

Fostering Innovation and Adaptability

Fostering innovation and adaptability ensures that restorative justice practices remain relevant and effective in changing contexts.

1. Embracing Technology: Utilize technology to enhance restorative justice practices, such as virtual mediation and online training programs.

The lips of the wise spread knowledge; not so the hearts of fools. (Proverbs 15:7)

2. Adapting to Context: Adapt restorative justice practices to fit the specific needs and contexts of different communities.

To the weak I became weak, to win the weak. I have become all things to all people so that by all possible means I might save some. (1 Corinthians 9:22)

The Role of Leadership

Visionary Leadership

Visionary leadership is essential for guiding and inspiring the church community to embrace restorative justice.

1. Casting Vision: Leaders should cast a compelling vision for restorative justice, rooted in biblical principles and aligned with the church's mission.

Where there is no vision, the people perish. (Proverbs 29:18)

2. Leading by Example: Leaders should model restorative practices in their interactions, demonstrating the principles of empathy, forgiveness, and reconciliation.

Follow my example, as I follow the example of Christ. (1 Corinthians 11:1)

Equipping and Empowering Leaders

Equipping and empowering leaders at all levels ensures the effective implementation and sustainability of restorative justice practices.

1. Leadership Training: Provide comprehensive training for church leaders on restorative justice principles and practices.

The things you have heard me say in the presence of many witnesses entrust to reliable people who will also be qualified to teach others. (2 Timothy 2:2)

2. Empowering Emerging Leaders: Identify and empower emerging leaders within the church to take active roles in restorative justice initiatives.

Do not let anyone look down on you because you are young, but set an example for the believers in speech, in conduct, in love, in faith and in purity. (1 Timothy 4:12)

The future of restorative justice in Christian communities holds great promise as churches continue to embrace and integrate these transformative practices. By addressing challenges, strengthening theological foundations, expanding restorative practices, and fostering innovation, Christian communities can create environments that promote healing, reconciliation, and justice.

Visionary leadership, inclusive practices, and collaborative efforts are essential for advancing restorative justice and ensuring its sustainability. As churches continue to draw on Paul's teachings and apply these principles, they can reflect the heart of the gospel and contribute to the flourishing of individuals and communities.

Through education, technology, and community partnerships, the principles of restorative justice can be woven into the fabric of church life, fostering a culture of empathy, forgiveness, and reconciliation. This transformative approach will not only enhance the internal dynamics of Christian communities but also extend their impact, bringing healing and justice to the broader society.

CONCLUSION

SUMMARY OF KEY INSIGHTS AND PRINCIPLES

Throughout this book, we have explored the profound teachings of Apostle Paul on restorative justice, examining how his principles of love, forgiveness, and reconciliation can be applied to modern church settings. Key insights include:

1. The Centrality of Love: Paul's emphasis on love as the greatest virtue underscores the importance of compassion and empathy in all restorative practices. Love drives the desire to heal and restore rather than punish.

And now these three remain faith, hope, and love. But the greatest of these is love. (1 Corinthians 13:13)

2. The Necessity of Forgiveness: Forgiveness is crucial for healing relationships and fostering community. Paul teaches that just as we have been forgiven by God, we must also forgive one another.

Bear with each other and forgive one another if any of you has a grievance against someone. Forgive as the Lord forgave you. (Colossians 3:13)

3. The Ministry of Reconciliation: Paul's writings highlight the importance of reconciliation, urging believers to be agents of reconciliation in their communities.

All this is from God, who reconciled us to himself through Christ and gave us the ministry of reconciliation: that God was reconciling the world to himself in Christ, not counting people's sins against them. (2 Corinthians 5:18-19)

4. Restorative Practices: Practical applications of Paul's teachings include restorative circles, mediation, and community dialogues, which help address conflicts and promote healing.

Blessed are the peacemakers, for they will be called children of God. (Matthew 5:9)

The Transformative Power of Restorative Justice

Restorative justice has the power to transform individuals, relationships, and entire communities. By focusing on healing rather than punishment, restorative justice addresses the root causes of harm and promotes long-term reconciliation and peace. The case studies and real-life examples presented in this book illustrate how restorative practices have brought about significant positive changes in various church settings and communities.

Through restorative justice, individuals experience personal growth and transformation as they learn to empathize, forgive, and seek reconciliation. Communities become more cohesive and resilient, capable of addressing conflicts constructively and supporting one another in times of need. This transformative power aligns with Paul's vision of the church as a unified body of believers, working together in love and harmony.

Encouragement for Continued Study and Application

The journey towards fully integrating restorative justice into church life is ongoing. As we have seen, education, training, and continuous support are vital for the successful implementation and sustainability of these practices. I encourage church leaders, members, and communities to:

1. Continue Learning: Engage in ongoing study of biblical principles and restorative justice practices. Attend workshops, seminars, and training sessions to deepen your understanding and skills.

The heart of the discerning acquires knowledge, for the ears of the wise seek it out. (Proverbs 18:15)

2. Implement Practices: Begin integrating restorative practices into your church's ministries and community

outreach efforts. Start small, with pilot programs and gradually expand as you gain experience and support.

Do not despise these small beginnings, for the Lord rejoices to see the work begin. (Zechariah 4:10)

3. Build Support Networks: Establish support networks within and outside the church to share resources, ideas, and encouragement. Collaboration enhances the effectiveness and reach of restorative justice initiatives.

Carry each other's burdens, and in this way you will fulfill the law of Christ. (Galatians 6:2)

4. Reflect and Adapt: Regularly evaluate the impact of restorative practices and be willing to adapt and improve based on feedback and new insights.

Test everything. Hold on to what is good, reject every kind of evil. (1 Thessalonians 5:21-22)

Final Reflections on Apostle Paul's Legacy

Apostle Paul's legacy is marked by his profound teachings on love, forgiveness, and reconciliation. His writings have guided countless believers in their faith journeys, offering timeless principles that continue to resonate today. Paul's emphasis on restorative justice aligns with the heart of the gospel, reflecting God's desire for healing, reconciliation, and justice.

As we carry forward Paul's legacy, let us remember that restorative justice is not just a set of practices, but a way of life that embodies the transformative power of the gospel. By embracing these principles, we honor Paul's teachings and contribute to building a church that reflects the love and grace of Christ.

Restorative justice, rooted in the teachings of Apostle Paul, holds immense potential to transform individuals, relationships, and communities. By emphasizing love, forgiveness, and reconciliation, restorative practices address conflicts and harms in ways that promote healing and unity. As we continue to study and apply these principles, we can build stronger, more compassionate communities that reflect the heart of the gospel.

May we be inspired by Paul's legacy to pursue restorative justice with dedication and grace, creating environments where all can experience the transformative power of God's love and reconciliation.

COMPREHENSIVE LIST OF BIBLICAL REFERENCES

- 1 Corinthians 13:13

- Colossians 3:13

- 2 Corinthians 5:18-19

- Matthew 5:23-24

- Matthew 18:15

- Matthew 5:9

- Proverbs 18:15

- Proverbs 22:6

- 1 Timothy 4:12

- Ephesians 4:25

- Psalm 34:18

- Galatians 6:2

- James 3:18

- Romans 12:18

- Psalm 133:1

- Romans 12:21
- Galatians 6:1
- Philippians 4:19
- 1 Corinthians 14:40
- Romans 12:4-5
- 1 Thessalonians 5:11
- Colossians 3:23
- James 2:1
- 1 Thessalonians 5:21-22
- 2 Timothy 2:2
- 1 Corinthians 11:1
- Proverbs 29:18
- Philippians 2:4
- Hebrews 10:24-25
- Proverbs 1:5
- Micah 6:8
- 2 Peter 3:18
- Ecclesiastes 4:9
- 1 Timothy 4:12
- Zechariah 4:10
- Galatians 3:28

Scholarly Works on Restorative Justice and Pauline Theology

1. Braithwaite, John. "Restorative Justice and Responsive Regulation." Oxford University Press, 2002.

- This book provides a comprehensive overview of restorative justice principles and their application in various contexts.

2. Zehr, Howard. "The Little Book of Restorative Justice." Good Books, 2002.

- A foundational text that introduces key concepts of restorative justice and practical guidance for implementation.

3. Marshall, Christopher. "Compassionate Justice: An Interdisciplinary Dialogue with Two Gospel Parables on Restorative Justice." Cascade Books, 2012.

- This work explores the intersection of restorative justice and Christian theology, using parables to illustrate key principles.

4. Wright, N.T. "Paul: A Biography." HarperOne, 2018.

- A comprehensive biography of Apostle Paul that provides insights into his theology and its implications for contemporary practice.

5. Gorman, Michael J. "Apostle of the Crucified Lord: A Theological Introduction to Paul and His Letters." Eerdmans, 2004.

- This book offers a detailed examination of Paul's letters and theology, with a focus on themes of reconciliation and justice.

6. Harink, Douglas. "Paul Among the Postliberals: Pauline Theology Beyond Christendom and Modernity." Brazos Press, 2003.

- An analysis of Paul's theology within contemporary theological discourse, highlighting its relevance for modern justice issues.

7. Van Ness, Daniel W., and Karen Heetderks Strong. "Restoring Justice: An Introduction to Restorative Justice." Anderson Publishing, 2010.

- An introductory text that outlines the principles of restorative justice and its application in various settings, including religious communities.

Additional Resources for Further Reading

1. "The Little Book of Biblical Justice: A Fresh Approach to the Bible's Teachings on Justice" by Chris Marshall.

- This book provides a biblical perspective on justice, connecting scriptural teachings with contemporary restorative justice practices.

2. "Restorative Justice in Practice: Evaluating What Works for Victims and Offenders" edited by Joanna Shapland.

- A collection of case studies and evaluations of restorative justice programs, offering practical insights and lessons learned.

3. "The Cambridge Companion to St. Paul" edited by James D.G. Dunn.

- A comprehensive guide to the life, writings, and theology of Apostle Paul, with contributions from leading scholars.

4. "God and the Victim: Theological Reflections on Evil, Victimization, Justice, and Forgiveness" edited by Lisa Barnes Lampman and Michelle D. Shattuck.

- This book explores theological reflections on justice and forgiveness, offering insights relevant to restorative justice.

5. "Paul and the Faithfulness of God" by N.T. Wright.

- An in-depth exploration of Paul's theology and its implications for understanding justice and reconciliation in the Christian context.

6. "Justice That Heals: A Biblical Vision for Victims and Offenders" by Arthur Paul Boers.

- A book that presents a biblical vision for justice that emphasizes healing and restoration for both victims and offenders.

7. "An Introduction to Restorative Justice" by Gabrielle Maxwell and James Liu.

- This introductory text provides an overview of restorative justice principles and practices, with a focus on application in community and religious settings.

8. "The Healing Power of Forgiveness" by Jean Maalouf.

- A book that explores the transformative power of forgiveness and its role in healing and restorative justice.

9. "The Politics of Redemption: The Social Logic of Salvation" by Adam Kotsko.

- An analysis of the social and political dimensions of salvation and redemption, with implications for restorative justice.

10. "Peacemaking Circles: From Conflict to Community" by Kay Pranis, Barry Stuart, and Mark Wedge.

- This book provides practical guidance on using peacemaking circles as a restorative justice practice to build community and resolve conflicts.

This comprehensive list of biblical references, scholarly works, and additional resources offers a solid foundation for understanding and applying restorative justice principles in Christian communities. By drawing on the teachings of Apostle Paul and the rich tradition of biblical justice, church leaders, members, and communities can foster environments of healing, reconciliation, and justice. Continued study and application of these principles will help to build stronger, more compassionate communities that reflect the heart of the gospel.

APPENDICES

DISCUSSION QUESTIONS FOR EACH CHAPTER

Chapter 1: Understanding Restorative Justice

1. How do you define restorative justice? How does it differ from retributive justice?

2. What biblical principles support the concept of restorative justice?

3. How can restorative justice be applied in your church or community?

Chapter 2: The Theological Foundation of Restorative Justice

1. How does the Bible support the principles of restorative justice?

2. What Old Testament examples of restorative practices resonate with you the most?

3. How do Jesus' teachings on forgiveness and reconciliation influence your understanding of restorative justice?

Chapter 3: Apostle Paul's Background and Conversion

1. How did Paul's background and conversion experience shape his teachings on justice and reconciliation?

2. In what ways does Paul's transformation reflect restorative principles?

3. What lessons can we learn from Paul's conversion for our personal and community life?

Chapter 4: Paul's Teachings on Forgiveness and Reconciliation

1. How do Paul's teachings on forgiveness challenge your current practices?

2. How does Paul describe the process of reconciliation in his writings?

3. How can we apply Paul's teachings on forgiveness in our church or community?

Chapter 5: Community and Accountability in Paul's Epistles

1. What role does the church play in fostering a restorative community?

2. How does mutual accountability and support among believers contribute to restorative justice?

3. How should the church address sin and conflict within the community according to Paul's teachings?

Chapter 6: Paul's Approach to Justice and Mercy

1. How does Paul balance justice and mercy in his teachings?

2. What is the significance of grace and redemption in Paul's view of justice?

3. How can Paul's approach to justice and mercy be applied in contemporary settings?

Chapter 7: Restorative Justice in Paul's Letter to Philemon

1. What is the historical context of Paul's letter to Philemon?

2. How does Paul appeal for reconciliation and restoration between Philemon and Onesimus?

3. What lessons can we learn from Paul's letter to Philemon for modern restorative justice practices?

Chapter 8: The Role of Love in Restorative Justice

1. How does Paul's theology of love underpin restorative justice?

2. What practical applications of love in restorative justice can be implemented in your community?

3. How can the church promote a culture of love and restoration?

Chapter 9: Overcoming Barriers to Restorative Justice

1. What are the common challenges and obstacles to implementing restorative justice?

2. How can issues of power, prejudice, and resistance be addressed in your church or community?

3. What strategies can be employed to build trust and foster open communication?

Chapter 10: Integrating Restorative Practices in Various Ministries

1. How can restorative practices be integrated into different church ministries?

2. What specific restorative practices can be applied in youth ministry, adult education, pastoral care, and community outreach?

3. How can the church ensure a cohesive approach to restorative justice across all ministries?

Conclusion

1. How has your understanding of restorative justice evolved through the study of this book?

2. What are the key takeaways from Paul's teachings on restorative justice that you find most applicable?

3. How will you apply these principles in your personal life, church, and community?

Practical Guidelines for Implementing Restorative Justice

Step 1: Education and Awareness

- Conduct workshops and seminars on restorative justice principles.

- Incorporate restorative justice teachings into sermons and Bible studies.

- Provide educational materials and resources to church members.

Step 2: Building a Restorative Justice Team

- Form a team of trained facilitators and mediators.

- Ensure diverse representation within the team.

- Define clear roles and responsibilities for team members.

Step 3: Developing Restorative Policies

- Create a framework that outlines restorative justice principles and processes.

- Involve church leaders and members in developing these policies.

- Ensure policies are inclusive and equitable.

Step 4: Implementing Restorative Practices

- Introduce restorative circles and mediation sessions to address conflicts.

- Use healing circles to support individuals dealing with emotional challenges.

- Facilitate community dialogues to address broader issues.

Step 5: Providing Ongoing Support and Training

- Offer continuous training programs for facilitators and volunteers.

- Establish support networks for victims, offenders, and facilitators.

- Regularly evaluate the effectiveness of restorative practices and make necessary adjustments.

Step 6: Fostering a Restorative Culture

- Promote restorative values through education and role modeling.

- Encourage community involvement and collaboration.

- Celebrate successes and share testimonies of transformation.

Additional Case Studies and Testimonies

Case Study: Restorative Justice in a Multicultural Church

- Background: A multicultural church in a diverse neighborhood faced cultural tensions and misunderstandings among its members.

- Implementation: The church provided cultural competency training, conducted restorative circles to address conflicts, and designed inclusive worship services.

- Outcomes: Enhanced understanding, strengthened unity, and broadened mission.

Testimony: Healing Through Restorative Practices

- John's Story: After a conflict with a fellow church member, John participated in a restorative circle. Through open dialogue and mediation, he was able to express his feelings, seek forgiveness, and rebuild the relationship. John's experience highlights the power of restorative justice in healing personal relationships.

Case Study: Community-Wide Restorative Justice Initiative

- Background: A community with high crime rates and distrust between residents and law enforcement implemented restorative justice practices.

- Implementation: The church hosted community dialogues, introduced restorative circles, and developed reintegration programs for offenders.

- Outcomes: Restored trust, reduced crime rates, and increased community cohesion.

Testimony: Empowering Youth Through Restorative Justice

- Sarah's Story: As a victim of bullying, Sarah felt isolated and fearful. Through the youth ministry's restorative justice program, she participated in a restorative circle with her peers. The process helped her heal and empowered her to become a peer mediator, supporting others in resolving conflicts.

The appendices provided here offer valuable discussion questions, practical guidelines, and additional case studies to enhance the understanding and application of restorative justice principles in Christian communities. By engaging in thoughtful discussion, implementing practical steps, and learning from real-life examples, churches can foster environments of healing, reconciliation, and justice, reflecting the transformative power of the gospel.

www.ingramcontent.com/pod-product-compliance
Lightning Source LLC
Chambersburg PA
CBHW071920150726
47999CB00001B/52